WOMEN
AND THE ART OF
NEGOTIATING

WOMEN
AND THE ART OF
NEGOTIATING

JULIET NIERENBERG

AND IRENE S. ROSS

BARNES
&NOBLE
BOOKS
NEW YORK

1997 Barnes & Noble Books

ISBN 0-7607-0445-7 *casebound*
ISBN 0-7607-1204-2 *paperback*

Printed and bound in the United States of America

98 99 00 01 MC 9 8 7 6 5 4 3 2
99 00 01 02 MP 9 8 7 6 5 4 3 2 1

FG

Acknowledgments

Our greatest thanks goes to Gerard Nierenberg, whose work on the subject of negotiation provides the philosophical framework upon which we built this book. Not only did he generously share his time and ideas with us, but he encouraged us to present negotiation seminars to women all over the country and abroad. His faith was the spur and we acknowledge a very special debt.

We are grateful to the seminar participants. Their input helped us determine the extent to which being a woman affects the negotiations: the strengths and weaknesses that women experience and a host of other data that entered our thinking as we examined the negotiation process and offered a method for dealing with it.

To our families and loved ones go thanks for allowing us privacy during the many hours of collaboration that isolated us. They made it possible to concentrate on the task at hand, even as we missed their company.

A special thanks to the women who attended discussion sessions, sharing their ideas so generously and giving us feedback: Janet Allen, Adele Chiarrel, Edith Finnell, Barbara Freedman, Jeanne Friedman, Mayrose Friedman, Maida Horn, Lisa Langer, Marilyn Nichols, Barbara Radway, Sheila Rossi, Elise Sherman, Gloria Zeif and Joan Zucker.

The office staff at the Negotiation Institute, particularly Judy Glick, Jeanne Kramer and Juliann Barnhart, could not have been more helpful. The endless revisions and requests for instant typing were honored cheerfully.

We can never thank our editors enough: Barbara Gess, who was painstaking in seeking clarity and whose comments were to the point; Barbara Wasserman, with whom we worked so closely and whose fine sense of order and meaning helped to tighten the manuscript so that our message was clear and concise.

To the above-mentioned and to all those with whom we've negotiated over a lifetime, thank you for the experiences that shaped this book.

Authors' Note

This book grew from a four-year collaboration in developing and presenting our seminars on Women and the Art of Negotiating®. Our ideas about the negotiation process and its relevance for women have been developed jointly, and we speak with one voice in presenting a method and a philosophy for making future negotiations successful.

As you will note, the singular "I" who tells a number of the anecdotes is not specifically identified. Because these illustrative stories reflect our individual personal experiences, it seemed appropriate to tell them in the first person. But since we are of one mind about the basic principles they represent, we felt it would be both irrelevant and cumbersome to tell you which of us is the "I" in each story.

Contents

Introduction

I was speaking to a prominent woman author one day, and when I mentioned my seminar on the Art of Negotiating, she visibly recoiled at the last word. "Negotiating! I could never do that for myself," she said. She is highly intelligent, productive, well respected in her difficult chosen field, and assured of her ability in her craft. Yet she lacks confidence in dealing with people. She even lacks knowledge of what negotiating means.

Unfortunately, she is typical of many women. Women are so often afraid of the very word "negotiation" that they do not even consider what it really signifies.

The truth is that we are all, men and women, negotiating all the time. Whether at work or in our personal and social relationships, and whether we recognize it or not, negotiation is a process that we use every day of our lives. As more and more women move out into the working world, many of our traditional roles and relationships are changing, growing more diverse and complicated, and new situations to be negotiated are continually arising. Choice or necessity compels us increasingly to be competent, equal partners in life and in the work force, and we can no longer ignore the role that negotiation plays in our lives.

While the process of negotiation is the same for both men and women, it is true that a woman often labors under certain disadvantages; some are inherent in her situation and some are simply her own misconceptions.

- She often comes to it with a fear of not succeeding.
- Her fear often makes her reluctant to assume responsibility for her part in the negotiation.

- Habits of acquiescence or the desire to please may prevent her from focusing on her goals.
- She may think it requires traits and behavior she does not possess (or even wish to have), such as aggressiveness and competitiveness.
- Very often men don't take her seriously, so she has to establish her credibility with each new negotiation.
- She may have to deal with male prejudices. She is expected to be competent, but assertiveness may be resented.
- If she is a newcomer to the process of negotiation, she is probably handicapped by her ignorance of its structure.

On the other hand, as a woman she may have certain unique advantages. Certain values which have traditionally been ascribed to women—concern for others, creating community, attention to body language, flexibility, searching for alternatives—are all essential elements in successful negotiating. Women often perceive these qualities as insignificant, or worse, as indicative of weakness. Yet these very traits are more and more recognized as important in the business world. No longer is the tough-as-nails manager sought after. The person who exhibits people skills is more likely the choice for a job in which relating to others oils the wheels of the workplace. Take heart if you believe that the sensibilities of the people you deal with are to the point. You're on the right track.

Negotiation is a process we all use instinctively; when used consciously, however, it can better help us fulfill our needs and pursue our aspirations. For those women who have been afraid to negotiate or who wish to improve their negotiating skills, this book offers a philosophy and a structure. It is our belief that everyone can learn how to negotiate successfully without violating the basic persona. If you use the framework we offer, you will:

- learn how to prepare for a negotiation, using our negotiation map as a guide;
- learn how to assess your strengths and weaknesses to provide yourself with a more realistic view of the personal hurdles you must overcome to achieve your objectives;
- grow accustomed to keeping the needs of both parties in mind;
- learn the importance of creating many alternatives, so that you never get locked into one position;

- learn strategies and tactics, how to use them, how to recognize when they are used against you, and the limitations of their use;
- learn to recognize subtle aspects of communication, body language and meta-talk, which will enable you to "read" your opposition more accurately, and monitor your own performance;
- come to understand the importance of creating a positive climate and recognize the power this gives you in the negotiation process.

Having prepared thoroughly, you will not go into a negotiation feeling disadvantaged, even if the other party is more experienced. As you gain more experience, the whole process will become more intuitive. You will recognize, often without consciously thinking about it, those situations which require negotiation, and you will initiate and implement the process more easily and with increasing deftness.

Getting a feel for negotiation doesn't mean that every negotiation will be a success. But it does give you a mindset that keeps you from facing bad situations with despair. And your increasing confidence in your own ability to negotiate will inspire others, even those who oppose you, with confidence and a willingness to solve problems constructively and creatively.

First Things
You Should Know
About Negotiating

Experienced Negotiators

You are already an *experienced* negotiator. You have been negotiating for your needs since your earliest days in the cradle.

When human beings exchange ideas for the purpose of changing their relationships, they are negotiating.

When you open your eyes in the morning, greet (or not greet) your bedmate, answer the telephone, travel by public transportation, carry out your multitudinous exchanges at work, tend your children, respond to your friends, colleagues, salespeople, strangers or parents, you are carrying on negotiations of consequence.

We negotiate *every day* in *every way* in *every relationship*.

Skilled Negotiators

The *skilled* negotiator recognizes that what we say and do has far-reaching effects on others. In other words, she is aware of what she is doing and why she is doing it.

The skilled negotiator recognizes that before we can negotiate with others, we must first negotiate with ourselves. In essence, this means observing ourselves in negotiations with others for the purpose of assessing and critiquing our own performance, and taking steps to improve it.

If we can evaluate our own personal attitudes, values and philosophies, take stock of our goals and purposes, look without flinching at our verbal and nonverbal expressions and behavior, and, armed with this new awareness, take a fresh look at the other party to a negotiation, we will be able to move the nego-tiation toward a favorable conclusion.

Finding alternative ways of talking about, reacting to, and solving our own problems is an important step in the negotiating process. Anything that changes you, the negotiator, changes the relationship between you and the other party to the negotiation and alters the outcome.

The complexity of today's world, the rapidly changing atti-tudes, the disparate voices raised from within any group require new well-thought-out methods of negotiation to produce agree-ment and understanding.

What is the right way to conduct a negotiation? Some people expect that a negotiation, like a scientific experiment or the trial of a legal case, proceeds according to systematic laws or sub-stantive and procedural rules. Face it, this is not the case. Ne-gotiating is an art. One can construct a conceptual framework encompassing the many aspects of a negotiation, but the outcome is dependent upon the variables involved, such as the individuals, the time and the place. However, learning how to use the tools of negotiation—preparation, strategies and tactics, verbal and nonverbal communication, questions, and supportive climates—will give you greater understanding of your own needs and those of the opposing side, and provide ways to satisfy them creatively.

Negotiation is a process that does not lend itself to neat categories of fact against which new evidence can be weighed and balanced like a mathematical formula. It requires a more creative kind of expertise. Instead of a "fair" division of the spoils, it can suggest ways of making bigger pies.

Our observations and research indicate that the methodology, philosophy, skills and techniques which we advocate in this book are applicable at all levels—interpersonal, business and inter-national—for women and men alike. In each instance, there are basic needs present in each of the parties to a negotiation. The skilled negotiator recognizes these needs and *prepares* to meet them.

Change and Uncertainty

"You cannot live the afternoon of life according to the program of life's morning; for what was great in the morning will be little

in the evening, and what in the morning was true will at evening have become a lie."

—CARL JUNG

Women have been variously told that: they lack assertiveness; they are too assertive when in a position of management or supervision; they fear success; men fear women's success; women can't make decisions; they make snap judgments and will not be persuaded by the "facts." There are mountains of Ph.D. theses and current best sellers to support these categorizations of women's behavior.

The fundamental error in each of these assertions is that they ignore change. They view human behavior as frozen, like a snapshot, and the image as projected for all time. Take a look at some of your own snapshots of last year or five or ten years ago and think for a moment about how much you have changed, not just physically but functionally and attitudinally. You are growing and becoming. You are still eager to learn and to change whatever patterns you may find in yourself that impede your development or interpersonal relationships.

Each situation is unique and will be different because of the special characteristics, personality, background and experiences brought to bear by the parties to a particular event.

No two people are the same. No person is the same on Saturday as on Friday. Things change. People change. Our responses to events change from day to day, hour to hour, as we have more input, exhaust one emotion or another, as our needs change or we regard something differently and simply change our minds.

Have you ever heard someone say, proudly, "Oh, I never change my mind"? Beware of that person in a negotiation. She will need special handling. On the other hand, we have often heard the phrase, "Just like a woman—always changing her mind." We think that characteristic, the ability to change her mind, indicates openness, honesty and a willingness to see new ways of looking at things. If this is defined as a female characteristic, we recommend that it be acquired, quickly, by all negotiators.

Accepting uncertainty is the beginning of flexibility and creativity. When we learn to stand with our feet firmly planted in midair, yet with aplomb, we can be sure we have become skillful negotiators.

Process Orientation

Bertrand Russell concluded: "To teach how to live without certainty, and yet without being paralyzed by hesitation, is perhaps the chief thing that philosophy in our age can do."

Margaret Mead, the noted anthropologist, came to a similar view: "A clear picture of the end—a blueprint of the future, of the absolutely desirable way of life—has always been accomplished by the ruthless manipulation of human beings in order to fit them, by the use of rack, torture, concentration camp, if necessary, to the decreed pattern. When such attempts have been merely the blind intuitive gropings of the fanatical and the power-driven, they have been sufficient to destroy all the values upon which the democratic way of life is based. . . . Only by devoting ourselves to a direction, not a fixed goal, to a process, not a static system, to the development of human beings who will choose and think the choice all important and be strong and healthy and wise in choosing, can we escape the dilemma."*

An awareness of constant change, a process orientation, can spare us from putting labels on ourselves or accepting a static picture of ourselves from anyone else. We need not be unduly harsh with ourselves. When we malfunction on occasion—make mistakes, trip over our own feet, put our foot in our mouth, spill gravy on ourselves or on another, fail to win the game or the case or get the contract—we can recover our aplomb quickly. We need not remain embarrassed or self-conscious or fear diminished esteem.

Not too long ago, I was asked by a friend to speak before a subcommittee of representatives of nongovernmental organizations to the United Nations.

I was enjoined to be brief, no longer than twenty minutes to half an hour, during which time I was supposed to present the nuts and bolts of the Art of Negotiating and Women. I prepared for the event over a long period of time, paring and paring away at the material which we normally present in one day. As I stood before the group, my major concern was that I would go on too long and I began to pare even more, leaving out essentials that would have made for continuity and better understanding.

*Quoted in *Science News Letter*, Sept. 20, 1940, pp. 186, 191.

Afterward, I felt my presentation had left much to be desired. Friends who were there confirmed it. I could tell by their body language that I had acquitted myself poorly, and what they said and didn't say reinforced their body signals. "It went well." "The audience seemed to be responsive." "They asked a lot of questions."

Not a word about *my* performance!

I had intended, but neglected, to talk about a process orientation—keeping in mind that things change and people change, that one is not the same on Wednesday as on Tuesday. Worst of all, I had left out the story about my friend Harry.

Harry went to parochial school for his elementary education. One day the teacher entered the classroom and caught Harry in the act of discharging a spitball. He was hauled up by the collar to the front of the room and made to write on the blackboard five hundred times, "I will not spit!" He was still writing after class, when the headmaster came into the room. "So, you're a spitter, are you?" the headmaster asked. "No, I'm not," answered Harry. "What do you mean by that? Aren't you writing, 'I will not spit' on the blackboard?" the angry headmaster asked accusingly. "Aren't you a spitter?" he asked again. "No, I'm not," Harry answered again. The headmaster's fury escalated and he said, "This is your last chance to tell me the truth. How can you tell me you are not a spitter when you've been writing on the blackboard that you will not spit?" "Because," Harry answered, "I stopped."

Well, Harry knew, even as a kid, that he shouldn't pin a label on himself or let anyone else do it. He changed, even as he wrote his punishment on the blackboard!

So, like Harry, I won't pin a label on myself. It may have been a lousy presentation but I have done better before and since and will forgive myself.

We suffer the tortures of the damned by asking such questions of ourselves as: Am I a failure? Am I incompetent to do this or that other thing? Am I powerless or weak? We must recognize that such questions create invented problems and that we can reevaluate the self-defeating mental images caused by such questions by negotiating with ourselves. We can look at the facts by asking ourselves better questions, such as: When or under what circumstances did I do this or that other thing that made me unhappy with myself? Did I ever do this or that other thing before, and, if so, under what circumstances? We then ask: What are my objectives? What are my needs? What are the needs of the opposing party (or loved ones, colleagues, employer or employees)? Can I reconcile the differences between us? Can I create a climate of trust, goodwill and desire to renegotiate?

With an awareness of change, a process orientation, we can look forward, not back. We need not play the same broken record over and over again.

We can be patient with ourselves and not demand instant results. We, too, are in process. As the Reverend Jesse Jackson said, "God is not finished with me yet."

"The only man who behaves sensibly is my tailor; he takes my measurements anew each time he sees me whilst all the rest go on with their old measurements and expect them to fit me."
                                                              —GEORGE BERNARD SHAW

Philosophy

Women of today have an opportunity to be more creative than ever before. All our relationships, institutions and assumptions about what is correct and proper, what "is" or "should be," are rapidly changing.

For centuries we were expected to follow the examples set by family and friends, with only historical figures to guide us when we dared to be daring. Our grandparents certainly never expected to see a woman in space and generally referred to their son, the doctor, or their son, the lawyer. In a rare case a family would produce a maverick daughter whose insistence upon becoming a professional woman produced considerable anxiety because it would "ruin her chances for marriage."

When, at age eighteen, I announced to my mother that I intended to become a lawyer, she was horrified. I was already married, so that was not her concern, "but," she asked, "why do you want to work so hard and worry about other people's problems? Why don't you become a secretary and save some money until you're ready to have a baby?" Despite her objections, I became a lawyer and found no other obstacles toward that chosen goal.

While we still hear a woman complain that a man got the job because he's a man and she didn't because she's a woman, even though she has more experience, we are just as likely to hear a man say a woman got the job because she has big tits and she's tall and attractive or because she's a woman and more management jobs have to go to women. Or, worse, we overhear a man say he's miserable in a job because his manager is a woman and he just can't work for a woman—something about the way they function irritates the hell out of him.

The new woman must relate to her grandparents, who may still worry about her virginity and marital status; her own children, with her expectations of them; contemporaries of her own sex, holding multitudinous viewpoints; the men and women in her workplace; and the man or men in her personal life. Are there formulations to which she can resort, which are applicable despite political affiliation, generation gap, or assumptions about the roles of the sexes at home and in the workplace?

We think there are such formulations to see us through the negotiations in all these relationships, formulations based on an underlying philosophy.

Our first axiom is that power and ability carry responsibility.

Our second axiom is that any responsible person is concerned with the perpetuation of life on this planet, handing down the wisdom of the ages to succeeding generations, and adding to that wisdom to improve the health and welfare of humanity.

Our third axiom is that our philosophy shapes the manner and style of our negotiations.

Have you examined your philosophy lately?

Each of us has a philosophy which, consciously or unconsciously, governs the way we look at the world, feel about ourselves and express ourselves to others.

If our philosophy is one of "me first, last and always," we can expect that our lives will be in a state of constant contention and agitation. No matter how captivating the veneer, people who don't like being used or don't want to be losers will fight back.

At some time, everyone has to negotiate with business people, bureaucrats, professionals, salespeople, friends, enemies and family. How does your underlying philosophy affect those negotiations? Can you afford to hold out for an unconditional surrender? Can you afford to fight to the last drop of your lawyer's blood or your own? Can you face the wrath of your children ten or twenty years from now if they blame you for the alienation of a parent because of the bitterness of your pursuit? You may lose more than you can afford to if you maintain a kill-the-bastard attitude.

Too many negotiators are steeped in the adversarial tradition. They want to win at any cost. They value the fight for its own sake. Their attitudes not only hamper and damage the settlement process but in the end defeat their own purposes.

Negotiation is a continuing life process where no issue is irrevocably closed, even after agreements are reached and papers signed. In a win/lose negotiation, the losers are asked to make a sacrifice without any apparent gain and have no stake in reaching a stable agreement. They are interested in only one thing: When will it be their turn at bat?

A me-first philosophy precludes commitment. Without a willingness to commit ourselves, we lack the capacity to be fully human and responsible members of society. Commitment means recognizing differences, but negotiating to achieve a mutual satisfaction of needs.

When negotiation is viewed from the everyone-a-winner point of view, new vistas open. Negotiation changes its appearance. It is no longer an offensive weapon, but a process by which we can achieve cooperation.

The complexity of today's world requires new, well-thought-out methods of negotiation that produce agreement and understanding. Both parties involved must gain and can win. The competitive spirit is necessary; instead of pulling apart, though, each side can enhance the other. Competition then becomes a cooperative effort toward common goals.

By this new definition negotiation takes place in a framework of cooperation, rather than of conflict. Its intent is to change relationships, not to widen or breach them. Differences of opinion do not automatically imply conflict. The objectives of a skilled negotiator are to solve the problems and create a better ongoing relationship between the parties.

The importance of each party to the negotiation coming away with needs fulfilled cannot be overemphasized. If we look back on our past negotiations, both business and personal, we will likely find that we negotiate with the same people more than once, indeed sometimes on an ongoing basis. If we have been able to achieve results in a supportive climate, this goodwill is significant to all future negotiations. It is the best guarantee that the negotiated outcome will be implemented and that the results will not come back to haunt us. It is this broad and humanistic view of negotiating that we offer.

It is our basic premise and operating assumption that an "everyone wins" philosophy should underlie every negotiation.

TWO

Preparation

"Chance favors only the mind that is prepared."
—LOUIS PASTEUR

The negotiation process begins long before the parties actually meet. All forms of training, education and experience are involved, as well as your knowledge of yourself, your philosophy of life, your career expectations, what you seek from the pending negotiations, and how you react emotionally and intellectually to challenges and frustrations. So, in a sense, you are always preparing.

However, as you approach a negotiation you can prepare yourself more specifically by considering in a comprehensive and structured fashion all the elements involved. And you can do this for anything from a short exchange during the course of a normal day's activities to a formal, across-the-table, extended business negotiation which may affect the lives of many people.

In this chapter and the next, we shall discuss the various elements of the preparation process, and how and why you should use it.

Negotiating with Yourself

Preparation starts with a self-examination that is, itself, a challenge, as you face yourself to confront feelings about the situation at hand and perhaps even how you feel about life itself. From such an examination emerges your philosophy and your understanding of the reasons for your attitudes, beliefs and actions. Then you are armed and ready to assume responsibility for your part in the outcome of any negotiation, whether it be business or interpersonal in nature.

The effort it takes to support a flagging ego is enormous. We hide infirmities and assumed weaknesses even from ourselves. We label ourselves strong or weak, good or bad, worthy or unworthy, either/or! But when we have the courage to look at ourselves, to self-negotiate, we are forced to examine our objectives, our fact-finding methods, our assumptions and the issues we've set up for ourselves.

Negotiating with yourself involves acknowledging personal traits and taking a hard look at:

- degree of fairness,
- ambition,
- assertion,
- states of repression,
- likes,
- hates,
- anger,
- guilt,
- joy,
- humor,
- seriousness,
- laziness,
- industry,
- ruthlessness,
- the way people react to you,
- the feedback you get,
- and beyond—the list can be endless.

The worthwhile benefits that will ensue from this process are:
- clarifying what you really want;
- knowing why you want it;
- knowing how important it is;
- how you'd feel if you didn't achieve it;
- knowing what you'd be satisfied with (settle for);
- the effects of the projected outcome, for you and for others;
- the rewards you'd gain and the price you'd pay.

You may ask, with justification, why you should negotiate with yourself. Isn't it enough of a challenge to plan the negotiation with the other parties? Negotiation implies changes in circumstance and relationships, and the prospect of change often causes anxiety—if you nail your own fears first, you will feel more sure of yourself when you enter the negotiation with others.

Maybe you're the type of person who doesn't suffer nagging doubts in the face of upheaval. Maybe you're a plunger and an I'll-make-it-work-for-me person. You're ahead of the game if you've been endowed with such an outlook. But negotiation with yourself is as imperative for you as it is for the self-doubter! How often we've seen men and women who spend lifetimes making things work, expending energy on keeping one step ahead of disaster and seeking victories against all odds, while not even benefiting emotionally from the endeavor. A little self-negotiating might have shown that the game wasn't worth the candle anyhow.

What if such a self-examination reinforces your negative views? Instead of clarifying issues and fortifying yourself, you may come to one of the following conclusions: that you are indeed greedy; the possibilities for a successful outcome are nil for such a wimp as you; the way people always ignore you, your chances of coming out ahead are indeed dim; you usually get what you want but people dislike you, your methods and your acquisitiveness.

What help is it to confront these unpleasant aspects of yourself? Well, if you were completely satisfied with yourself and your negotiating acumen, you probably wouldn't be reading this book. We believe that negotiation is the key to bettering relationships in all areas of life, and knowing yourself better is a valuable first step. If you don't like what you find you can modify your behavior. Facing up to your inner thoughts is worth the risk.

A Tale of Two Women

Two teachers were rushing to attend an important school board meeting at which a decision would be made about staffing. Several key jobs were at hazard and they were anxious to lend their support to the threatened administrators when the issue came to a vote. Traffic delays made them late and upon arrival, everyone was seated and the meeting had just begun. "You're late," they were told, "quickly sign in and be seated." They followed this directive and made their way to seats. The officers on the podium welcomed the audience and remarked that the impressive numbers in attendance indicated avid interest in the matter to be resolved. The spokeswoman then said, "A number of people have announced their desire to speak on this issue before a vote is taken. They have signed in prior to entering this hall, and will be acknowledged in order of signing in. Please keep your comments to the point and limit your presentation to four minutes."

Ugh! Signed in? To make a speech? Us? A moment of panic as they realized what they had signed, and the task that lay ahead for which neither was prepared. One quick desperate look from one to the other acknowledged their predicament and then each started to solve the problem in her own way. One woman quickly mobilized her thoughts and started writing her speech in defense of retaining the administrators' positions for the next contract period. So engrossed was she in this frantic endeavor that she didn't even notice that her companion had left her seat and quietly edged herself to the side of the stage where she presented a note to a person on the board, who handed it to the chairman. It read simply, "Please delete the names of Ms. A. and Ms. B. from the roster of speakers."

Problem solved. Case dismissed. Well, they had a good laugh over the incident after the fact and in thinking it over realized that one woman had reacted to the situation by negotiating with herself and then taking action, whereas the other had only responded automatically.

The speechwriter didn't think it through. Instead of figuring out whether she could change the circumstances she found herself in, she immediately tried to adapt and solve her problem within them. She did what needed to be done within that strictly proscribed situation. She didn't control; she reacted by coping. And it probably would have been an intelligent speech, even if delivered with a quavering voice.

The other woman had a quick negotiation with herself.

OBJECTIVES

Avoid making the speech; don't embarrass myself; handle gracefully and inconspicuously.

STRATEGY

Reversal: Hit it directly and quietly by writing a note that indicates a change of mind. Don't procrastinate; do it now before it's too late.

There is no impeccable right way. Both women took action to solve the problem. We think the party who negotiated with herself solved it in a way that reflected more accurately her own thoughts and needs. In pausing and allowing herself to assess the whole scene, determine her needs, and develop a strategy, she defined how she felt and acted in a forthright manner. We think her *action* was a more productive response than the *reaction* of her friend.

She was in touch with herself to a greater degree.

Self-negotiation, as it becomes part of your thinking, offers the means to analyze how you feel at any point and then consciously decide on actions consistent with your state of mind. This analysis is worth the time spent, and should become your habitual way of starting every negotiation.

The Negotiation Map

To provide concrete guidelines for your preparation, and help you focus on the elements one encounters in the negotiating process, we have designed a negotiation map. We strongly recommend that you use this tool because it forces you to analyze, in advance and in a structured and systematic fashion, the nature of your particular problem and how each element may be seen from your point of view and then from the other party's point of view.

The map (on page 32) lets us see at a glance the entire negotiation from beginning to end, allowing us to analyze both sides' views of the subject matter, clarify our objectives, supply techniques for thorough fact finding, isolate the points of disagreement, identify the many positions we may be taking in regard to the issues that divide us, and determine the needs of both sides. It also helps us decide how to satisfy these needs and forces us to plan alternate strategies so that we may be flexible in their use. (In the next chapter we will be discussing each of these elements in depth.)

This sounds like a tall order, and indeed it is, but we must go one step further in our preparation. Each time we enter a negotiation we will be going over this map *twice*, once from our own point of view and once from the imagined point of view of the other side.

As you examine each element from your own or your opposite number's viewpoint, you may find yourself reevaluating previous assessments of other elements. A recognition of the other side's needs may change your objectives. The subject matter may need to be expanded. Perhaps projecting the other side's strategies may move you to alter your own. You may be forced to review a multitude of possibilities you might not otherwise have considered.

Walking in the Shoes of Another

It is thus an important part of the preparation to give as much weight to the viewpoint of the other party as you do to your own. In an American Indian tribe, one piece of advice passed down from father to son was that no one should attempt to understand another man until he has walked for a moon in the other man's moccasins. Now, it's difficult enough to plan the stages of a negotiation for yourself. Imagine, then, how much more difficult it is to shift to a viewpoint that favors your opponent's needs and minimizes your own!

Yet you should do just that. If you gain insight from a different vantage point, you can expand the number of alternative solutions available to you, and be more readily able to produce the kind of supportive climate in which both sides can win.

But guard against losing your perspective regarding your own objectives. Many women err in this direction, but it can happen to anyone. The U.S. diplomatic corps limits tours of duty in a foreign land to a set number of years to make certain that American representatives do not forget where their duty lies, and whose interests they are serving! Perhaps women are prone to this kind of empathy because they view themselves as living in a host country—a man's world.

As a negotiator, your task is to see another point of view without losing sight of your own, but with a willingness to change your own if mutual interests warrant it. If you understand the other side's point of view and revise your thinking because you see merit in their proposals, you will narrow the issues and get closer to a satisfactory resolution.

It is very helpful to walk in the shoes of the other for:
• People who are inclined to make hasty decisions.
• People who tend to decide on a course of action without listening to the views of others.
• Those who are self-righteous and find it difficult to value the viewpoints of others.
• People who are so imbued with self-confidence in their decision-making skills that they don't make the effort to investigate sufficiently.

FIGURE 1
THE NEGOTIATION MAP

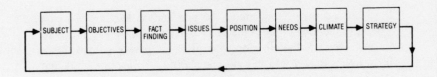

CIRCULARITY OF PROCESS
(feed forward and feed back)

YOUR SIDE ◄──────── Points of View ────────► OTHER SIDE

►SUBJECT MATTER 　seek agreement	►SUBJECT MATTER 　seek agreement
OBJECTIVES 　a. maximum and minimum 　b. expand objectives	OBJECTIVES 　a. maximum and minimum 　b. expand objectives
FACT FINDING 　a. assumptions 　b. hidden assumptions	FACT FINDING 　a. assumptions 　b. hidden assumptions
ISSUES 　a. points of disagreement 　b. major and minor	ISSUES 　a. points of disagreement 　b. major and minor
POSITION 　the stands you take 　　on the issues	POSITION 　the stands you take 　　on the issues
NEEDS 　a. yours 　b. theirs	NEEDS 　a. theirs 　b. yours
CLIMATE 　the atmosphere you 　　create	CLIMATE 　the atmosphere you 　　create
STRATEGY 　a. the overall plan 　b. the moves you plan	STRATEGY 　a. the overall plan 　b. the moves you plan

- Those who see pieces of a puzzle but cannot visualize the whole picture.

Those who are at peril in identifying too closely with the views of the other side are:

- Those who find it difficult to make decisions and who think their opponent is more skilled in this area.
- Those whose self-esteem is shaky and who might be inclined to devalue their own initial objectives when considering another point of view.
- Those whose need for approval might color any action that could elicit disapproval from the other side.
- Those who don't want to take responsibility for a viewpoint and would feel more comfortable with a conclusion by consensus, the facts notwithstanding.

Whatever your inclinations, do include the additional step of preparing the negotiation as if you were the other party. The ideas and insights you will derive from the task will be valuable in your proceedings.

Making the Map a Part of You

Although it may seem cumbersome to have to go through all these steps, particularly when beginning to develop your negotiating skills, this kind of preparation is essential if you wish to enter into a negotiation with more than a seat-of-the-pants attitude and a reliance on a tactic or two. It enables you to anticipate many of the surprises that come up in any negotiation. Used over and over, it will become so familiar, so much a part of your thinking, that you will go through it automatically, touching every topic and covering every possible contingency almost without realizing that you are.

You may not always want or need to go through every step. In mundane daily occurrences, preparation may be as simple as a reminder to yourself to create a supportive climate, assess the needs of the other, or decide what your objectives are, and it may take only a moment. But what a comfort to enter negotiations with the confidence that such a procedure builds.

While use of the negotiation map can and should become a habit, it is never mechanical. It is a flexible and circular process, and at the heart of it all is a philosophy—that in a successful negotiation, everybody wins. Putting this philosophy into practice means that satisfying needs, creating supportive climates, developing skills of listening and communicating, learning to recognize nonverbal behavior in ourselves as well as others, are the all-important elements of a negotiation, transcending in importance the old reliance on a particular strategy.

THREE

Elements
of Negotiation

Subject Matter

The subject matter of a negotiation would seem to be an area that both parties would already have agreed upon, but this is not always the case. Therefore, it's an excellent idea to define in advance what is to be negotiated. Do not assume anything, because assumptions may be false. For example:

- If I am negotiating to buy a business, I want to know that it's really up for sale and that the seller is not just trying to see how much it's worth.
- If I am negotiating to form a partnership, I have to know that the other party has similar intentions, and that he's not just trying to learn as much from me as possible so he can go into business by himself.
- If I am negotiating flexible work time, it must be clear that my boss is not testing me to see how serious I am about my job.
- If I am trying to negotiate a marriage reconciliation, I want to be sure my mate is not really seeking a divorce.

The initial step in preparing for your negotiation is to determine whether the other side shares your understanding of the subject matter. If you cannot agree as to what is being negotiated or even whether a negotiation is taking place, that is a cue that caution is needed and that the negotiation may be more difficult or complicated than originally assumed.

Objectives

Define your objectives! At first glance this seems positively simplistic. Of course you have to figure what you want from a deal!
Everyone knows that! Your objective is to get *that* job, *that* promotion, *that* person's patronage, make *that* sale, buy *that* house,
get *that* loan, get *that* person's approval. However, all too often
we tend to limit our objectives. By choosing only one or two we
may have closed our minds to creative alternatives right at the
start. Everything after that is downhill. Instead, urge yourself to
think of multiple, expanding objectives, with more creative implications. For example, you want that job—and a suitable salary
with adequate health insurance, preferably a pension plan, possible perquisites, the probability of substantial raises and growth,
the possibility of stock options to compensate for a lower salary,
the opportunity to expand the workload, or a flexible time schedule. Objectives can and should be expanded to the fullest. Only
then do you begin to see the possibilities in a negotiation. How
comforting to know that even if you don't obtain all of them, you
can achieve a good deal more than you had originally envisioned.
A cautionary note: In calculating your aims don't think of the
process as a fantasy session in which any notion, no matter how
outlandish, is permissible. That's only a good technique for gen-
erating creative ideas when done in concert with other brain-
stormers, because with a group to evaluate them you can have
some good laughs at the more ridiculous ideas and come up with
some workable notions from the best.

Objectives should be realistic, legitimate ones, not Walter
Mitty meanderings. Keeping them real makes them possible. This
does not, however, preclude expanding objectives and making
sure they are compatible with your personal vision.

Fact Finding and Assumptions

An essential element in the negotiating process is getting the facts.
Not only will you want to know as much as you can about the
subject matter in order to support your positions, but you will
also want to find out as much as possible about the opposing

side—reliability, track record, background, personality, etc.—so that you will know how to appeal, when to trust and where to be wary. This is only the first step. Next you must think about where the other party is coming from; not only must you determine the facts as *you* perceive them and wish to present them, but you must also try to anticipate which facts the other side will find relevant. Still you are not finished. As extensive as the fact finding may be, there is a dimension to it which we should never neglect. We must continually ask ourselves what assumptions are being made by both sides. Few people realize how much our belief systems are based on our assumptions.

Of course, we could not live in our culture without assumptions. When we hand the store clerk our money, we assume that he will give us our merchandise and our change. When we sign a release saying "received in hand the sum of $25,000," we assume that a check for that sum will come in the next two or three weeks. When we get on a plane to Chicago, we assume that it will land at O'Hare Airport unless we've been told Midway. If we had to test and reason through everything, nothing would get done.

The Role of Assumptions in the Negotiating Process

While we must make assumptions because we cannot possibly observe, check and test everything all the time, it is important to our own safety and sanity to remember that what we call facts are viewed through the lens of our assumptions. In entering a negotiation, you are severely handicapped unless you review your own assumptions and anticipate those of the other party. The competent negotiator recognizes that people often take positions based not on facts, but on what they believe the facts to be.

Negotiations may get bogged down if one or both of the parties assume that everyone else has the same perceptual experience—that everyone hears, sees, tastes in exactly the same way, or that there is only one right way to look at or feel about anything.

When dealing with strangers or negotiating with someone for the first time, we must make certain assumptions as to what their various words, phrases or body language mean. And we may be wrong.

When someone fails to look us straight in the eyes during an encounter, we may regard him as shifty, whereas in his culture it may be considered an insult to speak to a stranger without lowering one's gaze.

Even skilled negotiators may feel tense or ill at ease when their opponents are "different" from the people with whom they are accustomed to negotiate. Virtually any group can cause this unease—men, women, minority groups, borrowers, lenders, children or the elderly. Our assumptions about a particular group may be based on our own limited experience with the group or on what we've heard. Whatever way we come to these assumptions, it is incumbent upon us to examine them thoroughly.

Sometimes we know nothing more about a person than the company he keeps, and we may believe that is all we need to know! This attitude may put us in jeopardy, whether we ascribe positive or negative characteristics.

Example: A vice-president of XYZ Bank would frequently meet Mr. Adenoid in the company of some of his wealthy clients, either at their houses or one of the famous spas. After a time, Mr. Adenoid approached him for a substantial loan, which the vice-president granted without collateral. Mr. A. skipped town with the money and was not seen again. No one in the group of friends knew where Mr. A. had come from or where he went. Each had thought he was the friend of one of the others. On his assumed association with the group, the bank executive had considered him to be a safe risk.

In interpersonal relations, it is risky to assume that someone knew or should have known something because the information was imparted to a third person. If you left a message for a friend, doctor or lawyer who did not call you back, check it out. Your message may not have been received.

If you experience mismanagement, discrimination or harassment at some lower level of a company, find out whether these practices represent company policy. If they do, you may produce a favorable change in policy by going public with the information; if they don't, you may affect a positive result by dealing with someone on a higher level. In either case, a false assumption would get you nowhere.

Competent Fact Finding

We can learn to be competent fact finders if we ask questions that limit the response to a description of what occurred rather than high-level abstractions (judgments, inferences or opinions). Facts are limited to events that have already occurred. If you ask questions about events that may occur in the future, expect the answers to be based on assumptions, conjecture, inferences and opinion.

Good basic fact-finding questions ask for descriptions of what was seen or heard: What did she say and what did he do? Where and at what time did this happen? Why and why-not questions will be important when you are trying to discover the other party's needs, feelings, positions or interests. When marshaling your facts through published data, you should carefully examine the sources. Statistics are not written in stone and the other side may find equally weighty data that contradict your own.

Facts vs. Opinion

It is not always easy to differentiate between fact and opinion. A statement such as "He fired me" may turn out to be an opinion rather than a fact.

Annie was frequently found daydreaming at her desk or taking extended coffee breaks during which she was on the office phone making personal calls. She had been warned on numerous occasions that she was violating company policy by these actions as well as by her absences and latenesses. On her last day of work, Annie arrived one hour late and found that her desk had been moved up to the front of the office in the direct line of sight of her supervisor. Annie was embarrassed and angry and insisted to her supervisor that her desk be moved back. When told that there it would remain, Annie made one final retort, "If you don't move my desk back, I'm leaving." She paused a few minutes waiting for a response, and when none was forthcoming she removed her personal things from her desk and left. Annie applied for unemployment insurance benefits and indicated on her application for benefits that she was no longer working for the employer because she was unjustly fired. Annie had persuaded herself that she had been fired when the employer had failed to respond to her threat to leave. She omitted the fact that she had a choice and, in exercising it, had voluntarily quit her job!

Don't fall in love with your facts and assume that, just because you saw or heard something through your unique nervous system, it actually happened precisely as you think it did.

Limits of Objectivity

Einstein said "the light that enters my eyes is never the same as the light that enters yours." From that we conclude that no single event is seen exactly the same way by any two people.

We observe selectively. Several people looking out the window onto a busy street will see different events. A young man may see a pretty girl crossing the street, while a young mother may catch sight of a child stepping off the curb in front of an oncoming car. The observations we abstract from an event depend upon our interests.

The parable of the blind men and the elephant clearly illustrates the limitations each of us has in "seeing" what is going on. In that tale, each of the six blind men grabbed a different part of the elephant—and each described a totally different animal.

Each of us, with our eyes wide open, is like the blind man groping for reality. Each of us has a uniquely different nervous system, different capacities for sensory awareness, different backgrounds in education and training, and different biases.

Trial attorneys quickly learn this when they take testimony from witnesses to an accident. Even disinterested persons, reporting in all honesty what they have seen, will report substantially different or contradictory facts. A competent attorney will inquire about the weather conditions that day; where each person was placed near the scene; the state of health of each witness (what defects, if any, in sight or hearing). She also wants to know about the educational, social and economic background of each witness to get some insights into the reporting biases of each.

George Doris, who serves as principal consultant with a major London-based firm of management consultants, uses the phrase, "Where you stand depends on where you sit." This notion helps him keep in mind how the differing philosophies and biases of the parties on either side of the negotiating table affect their views of the subject matter.

We may have come to some "fact" because it is an integral part of the teaching or training we received which is believed not only by ourselves but by our parents, religious or cultural group, and the company we keep. Out of this shared or agreed-to belief comes our fact.

You may well ask how if we start from such differing points of view, can we get to see the same elephant? The fact is that we will never see the same elephant, but it is possible to improve our knowledge of how that elephant is perceived by someone else and, at the same time, enlarge our own perspective of that elephant.

Examine your own position first. How did you arrive at your point of view and your facts? How self-righteous are you in enunciating the truth as if it were handed down to you from Mt. Sinai?

If this self-examination causes you some embarrassment, you might well start the negotiation with a statement about your own doubts about the facts and ask your opposite number to set forth her facts! You can then point out the assumptions each of you has made.

Where the parties remain wedded to opposing facts but desire that negotiations continue, they can agree to be bound by the findings of fact of a third party who has been mutually agreed upon. This is often a primary responsibility of arbitrators.

You Can't Know Everything

One of the biggest fears expressed by unskilled negotiators is that they will be taken advantage of, suffer loss of esteem, or lose the deal because the other side must know something they don't know. Well, it's a pretty safe assumption that the other side knows something you don't since it isn't possible for any of us to know *all* about anything. Remember that the purpose of fact finding is not to make points but to establish the basis for a successful negotiation. Agreement on the facts is more important than whose facts they are. If you know what you need and want, and manifest an openness to the needs and wants of the other party, you need not fear that you will be diminished by your acceptance of any facts that have been revealed to you.

In preparing for a negotiation, do all you can to determine the relevant facts yourself. However if the other side's facts support the negotiation, don't try to hold on to your own.

As Dr. Kenneth G. Johnson, professor of mass communications at the University of Wisconsin, has said, "To convince someone, you must run the risk of being convinced by them."

Issues and Positions

We have identified objectives as the things you want to achieve. The positions are the stances you take to achieve them. If you can bring the other side to agree with your position, you're on your way to an easily negotiated settlement. However, where the other side does not agree, the item in question becomes part of the issue you're negotiating about.

The positions you take and the issues themselves should not be developed in a vacuum. The closer they are to reality the easier they will be to achieve. If your position is that your salary should be raised $10,000 in spite of the fact that the business is in peril of going under, you are being unrealistic and it will be very difficult to achieve.

The fact finding will show the areas of difference and may point to new issues that must be negotiated. Let's use an example:

• Subject matter—the sale of your house.
• Objective—to move to another town.
• Position—you want $200,000.
• Opposite party's position—will pay $175,000.
• Issue—how much will be paid for the house.

Another position of the other party is the right to inspect the house, a condition that you agree to.

You have assumed that your house is in excellent shape because you have had no problems with it. New facts emerge, however, when an inspector opens a floorboard and discovers termites galore! Obviously, the emergence of this new information may change your goals, the issues and every other element in the negotiation process.

This example points up what we mean by circularity of the process. You are never finished considering any part of the preparation. In this instance, your fact finding sends you back to reconsider your positions, and may influence your original objectives as well. New issues are born and the sale now hinges not only on price and suitability but on termites, of all things. You may have to change your position on price or pay to get rid of the problem.

On the other hand, you may want to *test* the buyer's position to see whether it has changed. You shouldn't make the automatic assumption that it has. Let your broker or attorney act as an agent with limited authority to ascertain whether the position of the other side has indeed changed at all. Even if the prospective buyer is hedging on the basis of this new fact, further fact finding may nullify the issue if you discover that every house in the county is in a similar condition, that it is manageable, and no serious damage has been done.

Locking yourself into a position is a trap in any negotiation. It is rarely useful, yet is particularly common in personal negotiations.

Because her sister Dorothy had not attended her father-in-law's funeral, Susan took the position that she would not invite Dorothy to Thanksgiving dinner. Hard feelings on both sides resulted, and they did not speak to each other for several years. If Susan had used the negotiation map to review the objectives and needs of both sides, she might have decided to express her displeasure without taking such a disproportionately self-righteous stand from which she could not extricate herself without losing face. Always try to position yourself so that you can change your stance should it become desirable.

But what can you do when it is your opposite number who has backed herself into a positional corner? Again, if you review the map, you will probably be able to address what is really at issue and take measures to relax the tension—use humor, assure her that you care, show by word or gesture that you won't say "I told you so" if she backs down.

Needs

Needs and their satisfaction are common denominators in negotiating. If people didn't have needs, there would be no motivation for negotiation. Satisfaction of needs motivates virtually every type of human behavior. If someone needs something and you are in a position to give it to him, you can negotiate with him. If he has needs and you are in a position to cut him off from the satisfaction of these needs, you can negotiate with him.

Having determined that a negotiation is necessary or desirable, it is essential to determine the needs of your opponent as well as your own. In determining your own needs you will want to draw up a list of priorities so that you don't confuse minimal or peripheral needs with those that are the real purpose of the negotiation. You may, for instance, want a promotion. You may also need reassurance that you are doing a good job. You should decide in advance which is more important.

Having decided on your own needs, look at the negotiation from the other side's point of view and, taking into account the personalities as well as the practicalities, try to figure out what their needs are.

One manifestation of the win/lose negotiator is that he knows what he wants but couldn't care less about the other side's needs. For a negotiation to have lasting results, however, both parties must have needs satisfied so that each has a stake in its continued success.

As a skilled negotiator, you will always be on the alert for signs of the other side's needs and motivations. This is an ongoing process that will flow from the preparation into the negotiation itself. The fact finding you have done beforehand should give some indication of needs. Then listen carefully to what he says and watch the way he acts. Try not to antagonize or create other barriers to the revelation of needs; as you discover them, you will assess their relative importance.

Abraham H. Maslow of Brandeis University, in his book *Motivation and Personality* (New York: Harper and Row, 1954), has described seven bundles of needs that influence human behavior. Arranged in a hierarchical order from most basic to least basic they provide a useful framework for studying needs in relation to negotiations.

Physiological (Homeostatic) Needs

Undoubtedly the most dominant, these needs revolve about the satisfaction of biological drives and urges such as hunger, thirst, fatigue, sex and the efforts of the body to maintain itself in a normal, balanced state. We cannot concentrate on the terms of a contract with a raging fever or a stomach virus. When we are confined to a negotiating table long past our usual dinner hour and we are hungry, our perceptions change, our emotions may become more easily aroused, and negotiations deteriorate.

A skilled negotiator attuned to the needs of the parties will prepare a positive climate by providing a comfortable environment, time for coffee breaks, bathroom facilities, and punctual mealtime respites.

On the other hand, a negotiator who presses every advantage may urge round-the-clock negotiations until those with less stamina give in or give up. If you find yourself in such a situation, remember that it is your negotiation, too. Do not accept deprivation and do not surrender in order to end it. Insist that your needs receive proper attention.

Safety and Security Needs

All of us are concerned with safety and security needs—personal safety, job security, etc. Job security may be very relevant in a negotiation. You may be concerned with achieving success in a negotiation in order to keep your job. On the other hand, if your opponent has put himself in a shaky position, you can take advantage of that. For instance, you have been trying to sell your company's dies to a firm in which the purchasing agent is a buddy of your major competitor. So far he has refused to buy from you. It may be playing hardball but you let him know that if he continues this way, you will have to let his boss know that he is putting his firm in potential jeopardy by relying on only one supplier for an essential part.

Love and Belonging Needs

Another major need is the craving for love and affection. While less important in the workplace, it is usually the dominant need operating in our interpersonal negotiations.

The mother of grown children who live away from home who constantly berates them for their neglect is crying out for reassurance of love and remembrance.

Some mischievous actions of children designed to get attention stem from the need for expressions of love and caring from their parents. Even reproach is better than no reaction at all.

As women, the dilemma many of us face today is satisfying the love and belonging needs of husbands, lovers or children, and at the same time satisfying our own esteem needs as we reject the traditional wisdom of "a woman's place." There are husbands who feel rejected by a wife who pursues a career. The refrain of the neglected wife is now echoed by the neglected husband whose wife works late at the office or whose travels keep her away from home. These situations often require very creative negotiation.

On the other hand, women may tend to make the need for love and belonging more important in work situations than more practical considerations such as getting the job done or getting a promotion.

Esteem Needs

These needs concern what we think of ourselves and what others think of us. In this category we find the desire for freedom and independence coupled with strength, competence and confidence as we face the world and its problems. It is also expressed as the desire for reputation or prestige, the striving for status or domination.

Obviously, satisfaction or denial of these needs can have a major effect on the climate of negotiation—for better or worse. It can also be used as a negotiating tactic. If an employee asks for a raise she may be satisfied, at least temporarily, by an assurance that she is highly valued even though the employer cannot at present afford to pay more.

Self-Actualization Needs

These embrace our desires and strivings to do our own thing and become everything we are capable of becoming. In lieu of a raise, the employer in the situation mentioned above might satisfy his employee with more challenging work.

The Need to Know and Understand

This need was long suppressed in women, particularly in relation to professionals with whom they had to deal. The doctor and the lawyer, for example, are still often unwilling to explain the reasons for a course of action that they are recommending, thus refusing to recognize this legitimate need. It is a need that women should be particularly aware of in themselves and feel the freedom to express.

Aesthetic Needs

We have a longing for beauty in our lives and some of us may even feel ill in ugly surroundings. Providing an atmosphere that caters to this need generally improves the climate of a negotiation.

• • •

Although presented in a descending order of importance, none of these needs is ever permanently satisfied.

Every business, political, national or international negotiation involves not only the institutions themselves, but the individuals representing them, and as such may well involve conflicting levels of needs. For instance, in a sales pitch, if you tell your opposite number that he might be interested in a job opening you've heard of in another company, you are trying to cater to his personal needs (at the expense of his employer) while at the same time trying to sell his company your product (which presumably will satisfy its needs).

As negotiating gambits, we can choose to work for or against our own needs and for or against the needs of the other. But if we choose to work against the needs of either, we must be aware of the risk. If we say to our employer, "Give me a raise or I'll quit," we had best be certain that we are indispensable to this employer or have another, better, job lined up. In any case, we had better have another job, as putting his back to the wall may make him act against his own best interests even if he needs you.

Understanding and application of the psychological dynamics of needs serves a basic function in the negotiation process. It is essential to develop this ability if you wish to become a skillful negotiator.

Climate

Some people have a knack for getting just what they want out of a negotiation and we never quite know why or how. We may not notice anything tangible that they do, but somehow they improve the mood of any situation and make everybody more agreeable.

They are masters of *Climate*.

Every negotiation has a climate. And more than any other single factor, this climate will affect the results of the negotiation. If you control the climate, you probably control the proceedings — for better or worse.

Climate is fluid and changing and requires continual attention. It is the product of many things which can shift the mood ever so slightly or, in a moment, completely reverse it. The personalities, styles, feelings and attitudes of the people involved, the difficulty of the negotiation itself, the comfort or lack of it in the surroundings, the way people talk to each other—all affect the climate. What is perhaps less obvious, but more important, is the role of nonverbal communication. Watch out for that sotto voce snide remark, that belittling gesture or grimace. Contradictory body language can destroy the climate. In our chapter on negotiating skills, we will discuss in depth how you can read other people's nonverbal behavior and monitor your own.

Effect of Strategies and Tactics on Climate

Negotiating strategies and counterstrategies are essential tools in changing relationships. However, as with most tools, they can be, and often are, abused, particularly when they are used to achieve satisfaction of the negotiator's own needs at the expense of the other side. Later in this chapter we will discuss strategies and tactics at length, and how to use them to negotiate lasting agreements that satisfy the needs of both sides. But before using a particular strategy or tactic you should always consider its effect on the climate of the negotiation.

Climates Can Be Positive or Negative

How do you feel when the other person is out to win and make you lose? You may feel angry, upset, challenged, defensive or even aggressive. How does the other person feel if she thinks that's what you are up to? Probably the same way.

Positive climates are generally accepted by the other side. Negative climates are resisted. They make the other party defensive and tend to stall the forward movement of the negotiations. A knowledgeable negotiator is always aware of the climate that she is creating or maintaining during the negotiation.

Not too long ago in midafternoon of a hot day in August, I was driving my car down a long, quiet street, anxious to get back to my office for a real estate contract. I could see that a concrete mixer was parked at the end of the street while workmen were repairing the sidewalk. Assuming that the cement truck was not parked in such a way as to block the flow of traffic I proceeded down the street, confident that I would be able to pass. However, I had not realized that another car was parked directly opposite the truck; trying to squeeze through, I got wedged between the two. I stopped, afraid that if I went backward or forward I would scrape the paint off my car or the other.

I sat back in a fury over the callous disregard of the workmen in blocking the flow of traffic and my right to pass. They certainly could have pulled up closer to the curb, and I wanted to jump out of the car and give them hell. Instead I took a deep breath and considered my objective. I wanted to get to work quickly. What would be accomplished if I got out of the car and blew my stack? The workmen would probably say, "Sorry, lady, you'll have to wait 'til we finish the job," and leave me sitting there. So I composed myself, got out of the car, went around the cement truck to where the men were working, and in as appealing a manner as I could muster said, "Gentlemen, please look at the pickle I got myself into! Can you help me?" The three of them stopped their work immediately and came around to the car, looked the situation over and backed the car out of that tight spot without damage and all the way back up the block to where I could proceed down another street. We saluted each other appreciatively, and I was on my way, no longer angry because of the delay. Only a very few moments had been lost, a small price to pay for the further demonstration that controlling the climate is the best way to accomplish the desired ends of a negotiation.

In the final analysis, you control the negotiation to the extent that you control the climate.

When you recognize that a situation is deteriorating and that you are angry, stop! Take a fresh look. Get beyond your own anger by using negotiating skills with yourself. Make the effort to respond with a positive climate. If the opposition is dogmatic, be creative, not defensive.

A colleague is after your job. She was certain that she was next in line for the position, when, to her dismay, you were brought in from the outside. She is out to make you look bad whenever she can. She reports adversely on all your activities. She recites with glee every mishap that befalls you, magnified out of all proportion to reality. She is out to win and make you lose. You are angry and want to lash out. *Don't*. You want to denounce her behavior toward you. *Don't!* She is a loser who probably did not get the job in the first place because of her poor negotiating techniques. Her sour grapes behavior will be recognized by everyone, just as your competence and unflappable restraint will be admired.

To become a skillful negotiator you must learn first of all to monitor the climate you create, so you can understand what effect it may be having on your opponent. Then you must learn how to cope with negative attitudes with which the other side may be souring a negotiation. There are certain basic orientations which, like the two sides of a coin, create positive and negative climates. It may be helpful here to describe some of these orientations, so that you have some general guidelines on how to create positive climates yourself, and how to deal with some of the worst climates you may encounter.

Judgment vs. Description

We have all met judgmental types in business or in our personal lives—the executive vice-president of the company, the clerk in the typing pool, or our own parents. In the presence of such people we know we are being viewed with a critical eye, because even when not verbally expressed, their judgments show in tone of voice, facial expressions and gestures.

Judgmental people know the standards and values everyone should live by, and if yours are different they'll quickly let you know about it. They ardently support the philosophy of their political party and have a pejorative label for anyone of a different political persuasion. They blame other people for whatever goes wrong; see no wrongdoing in any of their own actions; put people in good or bad categories; call people names and question their values and motives. They ask questions that begin with "Why do you...?" and "Why don't you...?" and make statements such as "My company makes the best widgets" or "My daughter is the brightest in the class."

You, on the other hand, try to eliminate judgments and replace them with descriptions. You make genuine requests for information. You report on events, perceptions, processes, feelings. When others make judgments you ask for more information, to learn what they've seen or heard. Your questions tend to be "What did you...?" rather than "Why did you...?" Your statements reflect an awareness that what you are talking about is an experience unique to you; you say, "To me, my daughter appears to be the brightest in the class." No one can take issue with such statements because you are acknowledging that what you are describing may not be recognized in the same way by anyone else. You are not afraid of humor at your own expense: "My company produced 30,000 widgets this year. We didn't sell any, but we produced them!"

When dealing with judgmental people, don't let them anger you. Remember that it is facts you want from them, not their opinions. You will probably find that there is very little substance behind their pronouncements. By asking basic fact-finding questions in a calm even-tempered manner, you may even help them uncover their own prejudices.

Control vs. Problem Orientation

Facing you is someone who needs to be in control of everyone and everything. He assumes that everyone else is inadequate or ignorant, immature or unwise. Therefore, he must impose his will, attitudes, opinions or information on others. He takes control by threatening or using any and all pressure tactics to influence, restrict or persuade. He negotiates his relationships in this manner with his staff at work and with his spouse and children at home.

This need to control is manifested in varying degrees. A parent might say to a child, "Nice little boys (or girls) don't do that." "You don't want to end up like so-and-so down the block, do you?" This tactic is called disassociation and makes use of the don'ts to dissuade you from wanting to be like, look like, smell like, think like or end up like any of those "others."

It can take on a more threatening tone in a letter that ends, "If you do not reply to this letter within five days of the date hereof, I will have no alternative but to resort to the court in an action for damages."

Carried to pathological lengths, the need to control may even turn sinister, as in this grisly little tale:

A newly married couple was riding off to a honeymoon in a carriage pulled by a nervous colt. At one point the horse reared up on its hind legs, interrupting the journey. The man took the whip to him and shouted, "Horse, that's one." They continued on a while and the horse reared again, pulling on the reins. Again, the man took the whip to him, shouting, "Horse, that's two." A short distance later, when the horse again stopped suddenly, rearing up and neighing, the man took out his pistol and shot the horse, saying, "Horse, that was three." The horrified young bride looked at her new husband and in a dismayed tone of voice asked him why he was so cruel to the poor horse. The husband glared at her darkly and said, "Wife, that's one!"

The control-oriented person is particularly difficult for most women to deal with. We tend to respond to this behavior with acquiescence or rejection. Some women are fearful of rocking the boat because of their emotional or financial dependence. Others are so sensitive to any impingement on their freedom that they will snarl at a man who offers to open the door for them. Anyone who exhibits these extreme responses needs to do some serious self-negotiating. Do you take umbrage too easily? Or have you allowed yourself to become too dependent? Sort out your own sensitivities before you try to negotiate with the controller. Then, as you go through the negotiation map, you will have a better idea of what control needs in the other person you may be willing to satisfy. You may find that he is willing to accept your independence in some areas so long as he maintains control in others. Of course, when faced with a totally controlling person, you may have to ask yourself if the relationship is valuable enough to warrant continuing. You may have no choice but to accept him as he is or walk out and cut your losses.

The person who is problem oriented, rather than control oriented, has her own opinions but believes in shared solutions. She calls meetings of her staff and keeps the group focused on the problems, not on personalities. She does not allow one person to define the problem for everyone but encourages everyone to explore the facts together, and she continually redefines the problems as insights are gained. With their strong sense of community and their drive to nurture, women are particularly good at establishing this kind of supportive climate.

Manipulation vs. Spontaneity

Strategy and spontaneity both have their place in a negotiation. However, the manipulative strategist generally damages the climate. While declaring that he is open, honest, has nothing to gain and nothing to hide, and no desire for control ("Trust me," he says), he is actually holding back information and real feelings. And when this form of manipulation is exposed, it alienates friend and foe alike.

You, on the other hand, let your motives and feelings be known to all. If you change your mind, you tell them you've changed. You admit your mistakes without covering up or blaming others. You ask for feedback and invite an open, honest evaluation. You do not challenge the other party's feelings or perceptions. You express your emotions as you become aware of them. You give others the pleasure of your joy and you let them see your hurt. If you are expressing anger or distrust, you allow rebuttal and reevaluation.

It's a good basic premise to begin with the notion that there is something of the manipulator in every new opponent you meet. Don't be trusting until that person has earned it. Have your agreements reduced to writing unless there is some greater good to be gained by not doing so and you have carefully weighed the pros and cons.

Neutrality vs. Empathy

A climate that creates a defensive attitude is one in which the other person appears to be neutral—that is, indifferent to anything you might offer and not particularly involved in the problem at hand. He appears cool, clinical, detached. He never shares another person's feelings. He is analytical, aloof. He will tell you that you have no need to feel bad, no need to be anxious or rejected, but will not take your side or exhibit affection or caring. In response to the question "Do you love me?" he will answer, "I married you, didn't I?"

This type of behavior is another form of manipulation or control, designed to keep you off balance and begging for a kind word. Don't get angry and don't fall into the trap. Do some self-negotiating here and see if you are willing to reassure your opponent in the area of his needs—like esteem. It will at least keep the climate positive.

Of course, the climate that we wish we could have at all times is understanding, appreciation and compassion. We want to be with the person who shares and reflects our feelings; who accepts us without trying to change us; who is warm, concerned, caring, respectful of our worth; who is sympathetic and sensitive; who listens and repeats what was said to show he was listening. This is the climate we want for ourselves, so we should strive to create it for others.

Superiority vs. Equality

His name and title on the door are sufficient evidence of his superior status. Nevertheless, he insists on pressing the point. He puts others down; he does everything he can to reduce the power, status or worth of others. If someone tells him he lacks information, he shuts them up. He tries to make everyone aware of his "superiority" in talent, ability, worth, appearance, status or power. He must be recognized as the best. Again, no need to get angry with this personality whose vulnerabilities are so obvious. Any little thing you can do to aid this constantly flagging ego will move negotiation along.

In contrast to this essentially defensive climate, you strive to promote mutual growth and autonomy. You are not locked into a parent-child, teacher-student, management-labor dichotomy. You see teaching/learning taking place both ways. You see both sides as helping and needing help. You seek to promote mutual respect and trust.

Certainty vs. Provisionalism

You meet an opponent who is dogmatic and intolerant. He is sure he knows all that he needs to know, that his opinions are right, and his ideas are truths to be defended. He tolerates only those who agree with him and punishes those who disagree with him. He expects conformity to all his rules. He makes it hard to breathe, let alone negotiate. How do you cope? Well, first of all, keep breathing. Deeply. It's the best way to keep yourself from exploding. If you can present your points in such a way that they sound as if you are agreeing with him, rather than disagreeing, you may even induce him to see some things your way. But it *is* hard, and uphill all the way.

By contrast, if your opponent is flexible, creative, innovative and willing to experiment, he creates a supportive climate. Attitudes and definitions are tentative. A problem is stated, input is sought, data are gathered, ideas are aired. The attitude is: Let's investigate, not debate; let's consider several solutions, not fight over the right or wrong one. Consequently, each side can benefit.

There are endless numbers of positive versus negative climates. If you can steer a negative or hostile situation toward a positive climate, you will take control of the negotiation.

Will you be considered weak if you don't respond to abuse with an angry rejoinder? A skilled negotiator realizes that you give nothing away when you refuse to fall victim to the other parties' manipulations. On the contrary, you are exercising control over yourself.

To establish the climate you want, you must be consistent and genuine. Your body language must not contradict the climate you wish to create. Despite your positive orientation and your best intentions, you may sometimes do something that offends the other party or makes them suspicious.

The first thing to do is put yourself in the other person's place and think of how you would feel and what kind of response you would want. Sometimes humor at your own expense can relieve a lot of tension. A heartfelt apology may well be in order. Taking responsibility for your actions is usually more effective and more acceptable than trying to cover up.

"Manipulative" is a pejorative label that may apply to someone who is out to win and make you lose. It cannot apply to you, however, if you recognize the value of positive and supportive climates and operate with the everyone's-a-winner philosophy.

Trust

When one party to a negotiation is intent only on winning and obviously wishes to make the other party lose, the opposition's reactions are predictable: They become defensive; fight harder; get aggressive; become more determined; or dig their heels in.

On the other hand, when a negotiator says that she would like to work on a problem without preconceptions and with the aim of reaching a mutually satisfactory agreement, a typical reaction is, "What's she trying to sell me?" The first approach makes a person defensive; the second, suspicious.

Another statement that makes people suspicious is "Trust me!" In other words, while it is of obvious advantage to the negotiating climate, trust is not so easy to establish.

Don't expect to be trusted just because you know that you're trustworthy. Trust is the end result of many interactions in a developing process. For example, each time we consider the use of a strategy or tactic we have to consider how it affects the climate of trust between the parties and whether it is worth the risk of damaging that climate. Establishing and maintaining a climate of trust is a test of a negotiator's skill. If you are trusted by the other side, many more opportunities for agreement will surface.

However, do not think that because there is a lack of trust, there cannot be a negotiation. Negotiation on the facts and the needs must take place even in the absence of trust. If, in an ongoing relationship, the other side has shown a track record of good intent and has consistently followed through, only then does trust build. At the beginning of a relationship there is no reason for either side to trust the other.

Strategies and Tactics

Up to now we have been following the sequence outlined in the negotiation map to build our understanding of the people and circumstances involved in the negotiation, and what elements will best advance its progress to a successful conclusion. Now we want to plan the strategies and tactics we will use. First, what is the difference between the two?

Think of strategy as the overall game plan which will determine the moves you make throughout the negotiation. For example, if you are seeking a raise in salary, you may decide that the best strategy is to convince your boss of your importance to the company so that losing you would seem too great a loss.

The short-term moves you design to implement the strategy are called tactics. Some tactics you might decide on are:
• Getting others to speak up for you.
• Presenting charts and figures to illustrate your efficiency.
• Emphasizing the cost of replacing you in training time, orientation, etc.
• Emphasizing the good relations you've maintained with fellow workers resulting in a harmonious staff who work well as a team.

If your strategy didn't seem to be working you might change it to emphasize your desirability not only in your present position but in the marketplace as well. In such a case your tactics might include:
• Actively seeking an alternative position.

- Expanding your expertise to attain the skills meriting a much better and higher-paid position.
- Setting a performance goal (i.e., ten percent more business within 60 days) in return for the promise of a raise if it is achieved.

At this point you may be asking, "But aren't strategies and tactics manipulative? And doesn't that contradict what you've been telling me about the need to foster a constructive climate and consider the other side's needs?" If so, you have recognized a true dilemma: Some strategies and tactics *are* controversial, and depending on the way they are conceived and used they can be beneficial or destructive. Furthermore, future dealings with the same people will benefit or be tainted by the use you make of strategies and tactics in your present negotiation.

In the discussion of strategies and tactics that follows, no attempt is made to assign a moral value to any of them. Your own philosophy, your ethics, indeed, the legality of an intended plan, will determine your use or avoidance of any one of them. There might be circumstances in which you consider the use of some especially adversarial tactics. Don't discount the possibility. They are all legitimate methods for inclusion in your inventory of possible negotiating aids. If this begins to sound inconsistent with everything we've discussed before, remember this—a sophisticated negotiator must be skilled in recognizing what the other side is doing, planning to do, or has the potential for doing. The strategies that may be used against you will be effective or not depending on your ability to recognize and counter them. But in any case, the importance of strategies and tactics is small compared to the needs and the climate.

Negotiators who have used a particular strategy successfully may fall prey to strategy complacency. If something has worked a few times, the tendency is to use it over and over. They are like people who have only one tool—a hammer. Every problem they see then becomes a nail. It is better to remember that each situation is unique and calls for a different approach. There are no pat solutions to a negotiation. Don't allow yourself to rely on any one technique. It will only keep you from engaging in the real negotiation, which is more complex and can ultimately be more rewarding than the quick fix a successful tactic will momentarily offer.

Overuse of a tactic stunts the growth of a negotiation, reaping results that are less creative than could have been achieved. Be alert to this trap, and view each case as unique.

Strategies and tactics are just tools to use in conjunction with other parts of your plan.

The same technique may be used as a strategy at one time or as a tactic at another. Some involve a proper sense of timing. Among them are forbearance, surprise, fait accompli, bland withdrawal, apparent withdrawal, reversal, limits and feinting.

Other techniques are participation, association, disassociation, flexibility, blanketing, randomizing, random sample, salami, bracketing, agency and shifting levels.

Let us describe some of them, and consider how they affect various kinds of negotiations.

Forbearance

One particular strategy, forbearance, is widely used in business as well as in personal negotiations. In effect, to forbear is to wait it out. Don't make an immediate move, don't state your position of the moment. Allow time to bring the other party to a change of attitude and action more consistent with your wishes. When you hold off, suspend, do not answer a question, caucus, or take time out to decide, you are using the strategy of forbearance. This can be very effective when tempers are high and a cooling-off period is in order. It permits the passage of time in which the parameters of the issues being negotiated may change. New priorities may emerge. A new mood may prevail. A deeper examination of the situation and its potential becomes possible.

Thus forbearance can sometimes move the negotiation along. However, there is a limit to its effective use. There is also a danger involved in diminished communication.

Let us examine these factors. Instead of taking action, you are waiting for the other side to alter its view. You should be using this time to line up support for your position, rally your forces, plan your next strategic move. You can assume that the other side is going through some similar maneuvers. However, unless after an appropriate waiting time at least one party comes up with something new, a stalemate can occur. So it is essential to be able to intuit when the forbearance is no longer likely to produce favorable results, but has instead become a liability. Nowhere is this more relevant than in close interpersonal relationships. When you realize that the limits to the use of forbearance have been reached, reestablishing communication becomes critical. Forbear too long and people become strangers to each other.

While forbearing, you must stay alert to the countermoves and strategies with which the other person responds. He has alternatives, any one of which might be effective. He can forbear in return, with a negative result for both of you: deadlock. He can withdraw, leave the scene while you forbear in private. This might force your hand if you're nervous about a permanent rift. He can change the equation with a surprise; bring another party on the scene to get a rise from you, enchant you with a present, throw a glass of water, play a joke. He may make your forbearance costly by canceling a trip you've both been planning if a dialogue is not renewed.

His reaction sets up a new situation that you must respond to with either more forbearance or another strategy. This jockeying back and forth can be a destructive game if the issues are not ultimately addressed, and if both negotiators are interested only in forcing the other to capitulate.

Surprise

A sudden shift of methods, approach or argument is calculated to throw the opposition off guard. It may change the center of gravity, cause anxiety or simply gain attention. In any case, you upset your opponent's sense of timing and, in the confusion that follows, you run with the ball. The surprise need not be a dramatic one. If you have been negotiating in a well-modulated tone and suddenly elevate the pitch of your voice, people will sit up and notice.

Think of the effect of combining two techniques, surprise and forbearance, in a domestic squabble. As tempers flare, issues escalate, and each partner tries to outdo the other in voice decibel, the combination of the two tactics might make a substantial change. If you lower your voice and wait it out, in effect refusing to contribute further, the argument might just wind down. Even if the tactic is met with suspicion, justifiable under the circumstances, it nonetheless gives an opportunity for a refreshing pause and incidentally indicates the wish of one of the participants to set things right. A calmer discussion could further reduce hostilities. Patience is the keynote here. If you use these devices, don't fault the other side for responding with suspicion. De-escalation is a much slower process than feeding anger, but if you stick with it you may remedy the climate.

There is a danger to the successful use of any tactic: It may sidetrack the ultimate purpose of the negotiation. If, for instance, as in the circumstances stated above (a fight between intimates), good results accrue through the use of forbearance and surprise, recognize that further steps should be taken immediately to achieve open discussion and genuine understanding.

Fait Accompli

This is a unilateral action, taken on the gamble that the other party will accept it. I once had an insurance claim for damage to some paintings that were sent to me from Washington, D.C. The examiner had looked over the situation and I awaited further communication. Instead I received a check, for a lot less than the amount I had claimed. But by that time so many phone calls had gone back and forth that I was relieved to end the matter by simply cashing the check, as they had suspected I would. They had effected a fait accompli.

I remember one dramatic instance of how an action-oriented principal of a high school used a fait accompli to respond to bureaucratic regulations. Informed that a new floor for the gym would not be forthcoming unless there was evidence that the existing floor was "seriously impaired," he took a hammer and chisel to it. "Now it's damaged," he pronounced. Fait accompli! He got the new floor.

Someone sends you a contract for signing. For the most part the terms are agreeable but one clause needs deletion. Rather than renegotiate the document on the basis of the one clause, you cross it out, initial the document, and send it back with your cash payment. Fait accompli? Maybe, but, if unacceptable, it might be an excuse for the other side to draw up a new contract with surprising new clauses that you hadn't anticipated, bring in their own experts to corroborate their reasons for including the deleted passage, or bring the document to a higher authority in an attempt to discredit your performance.

In today's complicated world, with its harried pace and an ever-increasing load of detail, the fait accompli often achieves its intent—to expedite your desires and sidestep red tape. But if you are thinking of using it, carefully consider the consequences if the maneuver should fail. It is a technique for those with a soul for adventure and you may have to bail out.

Bland Withdrawal

You interrupt the time flow of the negotiation process by leaving, sometimes without emotion or explanation. This is a highly risky technique that can put an end to the negotiation if it doesn't work. Before leaving the scene, whether silently or in a huff, ask yourself what you hope to accomplish. Your abrupt gesture is likely to confuse and probably anger the opponent. How do you plan to heal the rupture? How will you restore the climate? Will you regain goodwill, to say nothing of trust? Even if the tactic makes the other side more conciliatory how do you plan to work your way back in?

One incident occurred at a heated negotiating session in which one participant used bland withdrawal to make his point. This particular situation had comic overtones that were, fortunately, the means of resuming fruitful negotiation. Hoping to instill proper fear of losing the deal in the other side, the angry negotiator dramatically stalked out. And found that he had walked into a closet! When he sheepishly emerged a few moments later, properly deflated but somewhat amused himself, everyone in the room was rolling on the floor and this unanticipated slapstick achieved results more productive than anything his grandstand gesture might have. If only we could construct humorous finales to every such scene, how much easier things would be!

Apparent Withdrawal

Less risky is to withdraw from the scene, but leave a representative behind to heal the rift, plead your cause, suggest amends, and be responsible for reinitiating your participation. You have a degree of control although your opponent isn't aware of it.

If your opponent uses apparent withdrawal, remember that while his representative is trying to convince you to resuscitate the proceedings, he may be gathering forces to support him or looking to other deals, all the while tying you up because of your presumption (aided by his confederate) that he will, indeed, come back.

In this strategic give-and-take you might try to get a compromise from his associates as the price for reinstating him in the proceedings. Or you might use this opportunity to seek another buyer for that property. If you let him know of interest in other quarters it may increase his anxiety over possibly losing the deal.

Reversal

You do the reverse of what is expected. This technique has the element of surprise. Labor strikes are strong efforts to exact terms from the opposite side. In a teacher's strike, public opinion in an embittered community weighed against the teachers' demands. In what they perceived as a position of strength, the board stopped bargaining, hoping their forbearance would bring a quick end to the conflict. What they didn't expect, and what changed the whole equation, was the plan the union implemented. A token strike line continued but the bulk of the teaching staff set up impromptu classes in parents' homes so that the education of community children would not be disrupted while the strike progressed. This strategy of reversal—the direct opposite of what the school board expected—changed the temper of the community from hostility to a willingness to explore the genuine needs of the teachers. It did not automatically result in a settlement, but the board of education did come back to the table to negotiate in earnest.

Limits

There are many kinds of limits: those imposed on members of your own team in regard to what they may talk about at the negotiation sessions and for how long; those imposed on the other side; there are time limits, dollar limits, certain natural limits like a new season, an election, etc. And there are deadline limits— "If we don't reach a settlement by March 1, our new fiscal year, we won't negotiate further."

Some negotiators will institute negotiation right before a holiday such as Easter, on the presumption that everyone will want to conclude in time for the holiday. Labor negotiations at the end of a contract go to the wire, and a nervous public, upon whom the greatest hardship will fall in the event of a strike, brings pressure for a settlement.

The use of limits as a negotiating technique is fraught with danger. It holds an implicit threat—either/or! The option for developing creative alternatives to the proposals on the table is usually precluded when limits are set. Both sides may be paralyzed by the worry that the negotiation will fall apart once the limit has been reached.

The trouble with limits is that you limit your own options as well. You've issued a threat and if things don't go your way you have to implement your threat or lose your credibility. In the business world, it is essential to maintain your reputation for integrity. If you're prepared to walk and you truly accept that possibility, you may risk the use of limits. In personal relationships, you are less likely to be taken seriously if you threaten to walk out. Implementing the threat further complicates the situation but does not necessarily signal the end of the negotiation. If someone is trying to use this tactic on you, and you want the negotiation to resume, make it easy for her to back off and at the same time maintain dignity. Humor, at this point, can help. You'll think of something if you're not a victim of your own emotions, and your opponent will be relieved and grateful (even if she doesn't admit it). The restored climate can even be the basis for a more fruitful proceeding. A friend remembers an example of this saving grace from his adolescence. Disappointed in "love," he decided on suicide. His next-to-last act was to say goodbye to his favorite professor, who heard him out, said "I'm sorry," and led him to the door. Startled by the man's coolness, my friend waited a minute outside. Nothing, so he started down the stairs. Suddenly the door opened and the professor said, "Arthur, if you do this awful thing, I'll never speak to you again!"

Feinting

You appear to be moving toward one goal when you are actually moving toward another.

An effort to mislead may have several purposes.
- Conceal your actual intentions.
- Keep the other side slightly off base and wondering.
- Limit their ability to predict your moods.
- Give you time to pursue other options.
- Keep your opponent on hold until such a time as you wish to conclude the negotiation.

A famous realtor used feinting to conclude many an important real estate transaction. Approached to find a site for a large development, he was able to assemble the land from small-business owners who never suspected his true plans for it. Had they been aware, they might have held out individually, or joined together to obtain much more money for their properties. How did he mislead them? He leaked to the press his intention of securing a large site near the Hudson River, directly across town from their neighborhood. So swiftly were the parcels assembled that his feinting strategy paid off and the complex now stands where they used to do business.

Before she approached her boss for a raise, my friend Betty made certain that he knew that other jobs had been offered her, any one of which would provide more remuneration than her present situation. She really wanted to stay where she was and she would have been willing to do so even if she hadn't achieved her aim of more compensation. But she made him believe that he would have to match or better what she could get elsewhere. He matched it, and so her feinting strategy worked.

This widely used old ploy is almost a cliché. Yet a little deception about intentions is often effective, especially at the beginning of a negotiation, when the very nature of what's being negotiated is still in doubt and relationships have yet to be established. In the preliminary dance, when each side is testing the other and trying to fathom how much strength the opponent has, it's a legitimate modus operandi. In any protracted negotiation, this sort of bluffing gives way to a more genuine assessment of the facts involved, the true issues, and the needs that have to be addressed.

Feinting precludes saying what you mean and is anathema to true communication. In interpersonal relationships, little is gained by using this technique. You will be recognized as someone whose pronounced intentions cannot be relied upon. The air of mystery you generate will not build trust. It is better to find the means to a direct and genuine expression of your feelings and desires.

Favors

There will be instances during a negotiation when the other party asks for a favor: I need a week more for shipping the merchandise. Can we move the meeting up to 10 A.M. on Friday? I've got to make a revision in the contract; will you agree to delete article 5?

Some negotiators, when they are in a position to grant a request, believe that their gracious act is more likely to gain appreciation if the other side realizes that a favor is being bestowed. The element of timing is a consideration. Favors too easily granted may give the impression that they are insignificant and therefore not worthy of a show of gratitude. The calculated tactic of pausing, pointing out the inconvenience such an act would cause, but then granting the request gives importance to your generosity and will hopefully gain the appreciation meriting a favor or concession in return. You say, "I'd like to change the meeting time, but my other appointments present a conflict and Jane is scheduled to leave for Boston that morning.... It's a hassle.... Let me see what I can do.... I'll have to get back to you." When you call an hour later to say that you have miraculously made it all come together for his convenience, he will be properly grateful. Or will he? Such a manipulative tactic has attendant risks. What makes you think the opposing party will not see through your ruse and resent you, no matter how outwardly pleased he appears? Another consideration is the hostility engendered when one is beholden to another. Far from expecting this person to respond with a generous act in return, you might be surprised to learn that none is forthcoming.

In a personal situation, temporarily withholding a favor that can be readily granted only causes anxiety. Attend to the climate that nurtures a relationship and give ready reassurance. Make haste to grant whatever wish it's in your power to grant, not to garner personal points but for the welfare of the negotiating climate.

Anger and Intimidation

Anger, whether real or feigned, is often used as a tactic in a negotiation. How does it work, and what does it accomplish?

For one thing, the person displaying the anger may be trying to convince the other side of the seriousness of his position. And inexperienced negotiators may indeed be affected by an assault. If you are unaccustomed to such behavior it may get you to reconsider the reasonableness and feasibility of your position. That is its calculated purpose. However, any technique has an uncertain outcome. Instead of getting you to relinquish a point, anger may only strengthen your desire to resist.

If you are considering use of intimidation to achieve quick concessions, think again. When a person feels threatened, overwhelmed, embarrassed, uncomfortable or inadequate, he will very likely counterattack, especially if the tactic is recognized for what it is—a calculated move to gain a point. It is more in the nature of a power play and that's not what negotiation is all about.

Participation

Enlist the help of others to work in your behalf.

Do you remember how Tom Sawyer got that fence painted? He made it seem like fun and gained enough volunteers to get the job done in record time.

If strategies and tactics are manipulative, the use of participation is one of the more acceptable forms of manipulation.

I was traveling to California to do a series of seminars but I had to make an overnight stop in Chicago. It occurred to me that sending a carton of heavy books right on to California would save much wear and tear. I congratulated myself on having doped out this scheme in time to implement it. Usually these wonderful ideas occur to me after the fact and leave me wondering, why didn't I think of that before? It didn't occur to me that my brilliant idea would meet with resistance but such was the case when I approached the ticket agent, who arbitrarily informed me that the books would have to debark with me at Chicago. "The rules" forbade sending hand luggage on ahead.

Such bureaucratic mandates are infuriating, particularly because so often they're at the expense of the customer and his comfort. Sometimes life is a laboratory, however, and this was such an instance. Instead of escalating the anger I was feeling— and simply reacting to this uncompromising behavior—I negotiated. It was only after the fact that I realized I had used the technique of participation. I asked the ticket agent, in a conspiratorial tone calculated to encourage his interest, "If this were your problem, how would you handle it?" Immediately his attitude changed. Now party to the problem, he thought for a moment, and then said, "If this were my problem, I'd say I was going to California, and watch my bags go down the luggage chute. Then I would say, 'I changed my mind, I think I'll get off at Chicago first.' By that time the luggage would have gone on to California, and you would simply pick it up later when you arrived."

"That's a fantastic idea. Can you do that for me?"

"Sure," he said, "no problem." Thus his participation in my dilemma paid off by solving my problem and giving his ego a boost as well.

Participation can be successful if a situation demands its use. Don't expect it to work if you resort to it so often that people feel used and manipulated.

Association

You get prominent, knowledgeable, influential or "beautiful" people to endorse your stand. Or you attempt to enhance your power image by acting like, or keeping company with, the rich and famous.

If Woody Allen sups at Elaine's restaurant, I shall, too. If Sophia Loren, Gloria Swanson and a host of other legendary figures wear mink, why not me? How many charity contributions are made on the strength of which prominent figures are on the board? The lure and the glamour of the famous and exalted are an incentive to participate with them in causes, in pleasures, in taste. (Con men are well aware of this.) In a negotiation you might think it to your advantage to let the other side know you went to an Ivy League school. But this can boomerang if your opponent was rejected by Harvard and has never quite gotten over it.

Disassociation

By the same token, we prefer to disassociate ourselves from the unsavory, the criminal, the "losers" of society. This occurs in business as well as on a personal level. One suspects that the American Tobacco Company changed its name to American Brands in an attempt to disassociate from the damaging connotation of cigarettes.

We indulge our personal prejudices by separating *us* from *them* and putting psychological distance between. Such elitism is calculated to gain a psychological advantage. It may accomplish this goal by making an opposite negotiator ill at ease but such a maneuver destroys the climate.

Statistical Data

Statistical data—polls, random samples, etc.—are often used to reinforce a position and they can indeed be very impressive and persuasive. However, if you don't know how it's been derived, you can be misled. If I read that 85 percent of the Canadian people are in favor of smoking marijuana, it would be of great interest to me to know that the random sample was derived by analyzing data obtained only from youth hostels across Canada.

If you hope to strengthen your own position with figures, remember that they are easily checked and invalidated if false or irrelevant. As a competent negotiator, you also want to check the source of the other side's statistics.

Salami

Take a small piece at a time until you have the whole salami. This technique requires stamina. Breaking down what you want into smaller bites necessitates many small negotiations calculated to wear down the other side, gain concession after concession, until you achieve your goal—the whole salami! Kids are adept at this tactic, as any parent trying to put a child to sleep can attest: Can you read me a story? Just one more—please. I have to go to the bathroom. I'm thirsty. I've got a tummy ache. Kiss me goodnight. Can I just listen to one program? And so on, until their own fatigue wears them out. If your aim is to create a climate of respect and goodwill, be warned that use of this tactic will cause the other party to feel manipulated and determined not to fall prey to you ever again.

A simple "no" can suffice. Setting strict limits is a counter. Showing that you recognize what your opponent is doing can put a halt to that one more request.

The creative negotiator uses the salami tactic in reverse. Instead of taking small bites, she adds dimensions and creates a bigger salami. A salesperson can increase the scope of the sale: "Let me show you the shoes that would be great with that outfit; we also have matching slacks to make a whole other look."

Bracketing

This fact-finding technique can be used tactically. It takes its name from the old military practice of firing the first shot over the target and the second shot under the target, then calculating the difference to hit on target. For instance, a sales rep might say to his customer, "I know you'd never get this fabric for $10 a yard." When he's registered the expression in the customer's eyes he adds, "I hear my competitor's asking $12." He then offers a figure in between, based on what he judges the client will consider advantageous as well as his own need to make a profit.

Changing Levels

When negotiations have taken a bad turn or perhaps even stalemated, it's not unusual to be so discouraged that you stop looking for alternatives. At such times it is valuable to remember the tactic of changing levels. You raise or lower your viewpoint—appeal to someone in a position of higher authority for input or to mediate, or go directly to the crew working under you to gain support for your position and add strength to your cause. For instance, the workers in your small business are being urged by their union to strike—plead your cause with the parent union to get their aid in forestalling what you feel will be an unfortunate undertaking.

Silence

Silence as an effective negotiating tool depends on how you use it.

Writing about Dashiell Hammett in *The New York Times* of October 5, 1983, Christopher Lehmann-Haupt gave an example of silence used destructively. "Silence was Hammett's weapon—silence turned against all bullies and lovers, against his readers and himself. At the bottom of that silence was an ocean of anger."

Silence can be a blessing also. You've done something wrong. They know it, you know they know. They maintain silence and, because they don't scold, you are able to save face.

In some instances, if you hold your tongue it forces the other side to continue talking. People are uncomfortable with silence and will tend to fill the gap: "I think $4,000 is a fair settlement." Silence. "My client can't go higher than $4,500." Silence. "Maybe

I can get her to pay the interest on the loan." And so on. Of course, a skilled negotiator would want to probe the reasons for the silence to discover that perhaps she got no reaction because she wasn't understood. Again, asking the right question, such as "What is your feeling about my last offer?" is the key to obtaining this information.

Low Balling

If ever you think you're going to make a killing, think again—and try to figure out the strategy the other side is using. A car salesman offers just the car you're after at a ridiculously low price. If you fall for it you deserve the bad news that he can't possibly deliver, and after you've committed yourself he'll switch you to another car, more realistically priced. A counter to this strategy of low balling lies in doing your homework before you get to the buying stage. What is a realistic price and what should be included in it? What's the date of expected delivery? Warranties? Get it in writing. Make sure witnesses are present. Nail him to his agreement if you decide you want to go ahead.

A contractor's bid is lower by far than any other you've had. Ask how he arrived at the price. You can understand the figures better if the costs are broken down: material, time, labor. Oddly enough, buyers seldom ask for this and therefore lack a basis for judgment. If the potential worker balks at your requests, something's amiss. Reconsider whether you want to give him the job. Check with his satisfied cutomers, too. He should be pleased to give you references to call.

Flexibility

It is important to remember that you can use combinations of strategies or seek alternatives when your actions are netting negative results. Too often one tends to nag habitually, or yell and scream over and over, or continually issue ultimatums even when it brings nothing but resistance. A negotiator's first task is to take a hard look at herself so as to recognize patterns of action that persist and to analyze results therefrom. If you are forced to admit that you have a specific bag of tricks that get pulled out to meet any occasion, think about all the other alternatives that are available. Whatever your results are now, if your habit has been to react to situations with a few limited methods, a wider range of action could undoubtedly bring better and more satisfying results.

If You're a Woman It's Different

Women legitimately use all these strategies and tactics but they often get different reactions from both men and women than would have ensued if the maneuver had been initiated by a man. For instance, in the calculated use of anger to gain a concession, women often have more difficulty carrying it off, if indeed they opt to use it at all. Aggressive behavior is more shocking when exercised by women and evokes stronger reactions. Instead of achieving the desired result, it may cause a man to strike back hard in an effort to put an end to such a tactic. And often a woman will back down in the face of an onslaught where a man might stand his ground. Such was the case at a faculty meeting in which an irate woman professor strongly expressed a minority view, only to be upbraided and told to sit down. A man would not likely have acquiesced in embarrassed silence as she did.

Practice and Pitfalls

In a formal negotiation, when a team gets together to prepare, strategies and tactics are considered for use during the negotiation. They are used separately or in combination and can be changed during the negotiation if they're not effective.

Tactics and strategies are useful as tools, but it is important to guard against getting too caught up in them. They are effective only so long as you keep them in perspective and remember the dangers inherent in their use:

• They are easily recognized and often easily countered.
• If recognized as manipulative, they are resented.
• They generally serve the needs of one side, but not the other.
• They can destroy the climate.
• Sometimes they are downright dirty.
• Or even illegal!

But, nonetheless, you must plan strategy and, even more important, you must assess the strategy that the other side may be using so you can adequately deal with it. If you can recognize a style, you'll be likely to see it repeated over and over by the same negotiator. This can work to your advantage, particularly if you are skilled in the total negotiation process and deal with the more significant elements of needs, facts, assumptions, and climate. Strategy alone does not a negotiation make!

In personal relationships, one is well advised to deemphasize the use of strategy and tactics in favor of establishing a positive climate in which true needs can be addressed and solutions created to meet them. This is a harder and more taxing road—but the results are longer-lasting and make relationships grow.

In the final analysis one's philosophy and morality determines which strategies and tactics are permissible. It is a personal decision each time and one that deserves consideration at each new negotiation.

A Short-Form Negotiation Map

Most negotiations are on-the-spot occurrences for which you can't prepare thoroughly. Your boss is screaming about a misplaced file and blaming you unfairly for its disappearance. In such an instance you need to resolve the negotiation *on the spot*. It is helpful to keep in mind a short form of the map so that you can react quickly.

OBJECTIVES	NEEDS	CLIMATE

OBJECTIVES
- Find the file.
- Keep your job.
- Get him to cool down.
- If possible, save face for both of you.

Focus on what you want to achieve and you'll refrain from actions that get opposite results.

NEEDS
You want to keep this job and this security need has higher priority than fulfilling esteem needs or salving your wounded pride. Force yourself to think of what needs your boss has, and what's at stake for him if that file isn't retrieved. Will he lose the account? Will

he miss the deadline? Is *his* job in jeopardy? Changing your level of thinking to see the situation from his point of view will make you feel more cooperative and therefore more focused on the objective of finding the file.

CLIMATE

Expressing your anger or refusing to cooperate because you've been humiliated is counterproductive at the moment. Hold those feelings in check—forbear. Showing concern for the problem at hand and doing what *you* can to solve it will reassure your boss, ameliorate his frustration, and probably calm yourself as well. In other words, you will have improved the climate. When he is calmer he will be better able to recognize that you were not responsible for the mishap.

Remember, for situations that demand instant negotiation, think: objectives, needs and climate.

FOUR

The Negotiating Skills

Every human being starts from birth as a novice negotiator. We are compelled to negotiate for the fulfillment of our needs from our first cries for milk and our early temper tantrums in response to "no."

However, at some period in development, many people make a conscious attempt to deal with negotiations thoughtfully. As novices they learn the vocabulary of negotiation and attempt to understand its subject matter. Often, however, in negotiation with more experienced people, novices have a hard time concluding or even beginning the negotiation. They may be subjected to unfair or drastic demands, or barely concealed hostility or contempt. One common reason is that, having mastered the vocabulary and some knowledge of a subject—real estate, for example—novices think they are ready to negotiate a deal. Not so. Negotiating and real estate involve two different vocabularies and information systems. There is a danger in assuming that expertise in one can be carried over to the other. One must prove competence in *both* systems in order to negotiate successfully.

The Pause for Reflection

Unless you are like Will Rogers, who "never met a man I didn't like," in the course of a lifetime you are apt to meet behavorial types who arouse fear, rage, helplessness and a host of other unpleasant emotions, people whose greatest delight is to frustrate, thwart or annoy others. In some instances, the flight or fight reflex (ducking, running, screaming, struggling against the attacker) may save your life. In less extreme situations, however, if you don't allow anyone to push your buttons, you can counter any defensive or negative climate that comes your way. That is not to say that an expression of anger would not be an appropriate response in a particular situation. Such response, however, would hopefully follow a pause for reflection. During the reflective moment reason takes control of the emotions and a whole gamut of possibilities is run through the mental computer. In that instant, it is wise to review your own objectives to see how they can best be served. Don't respond in a way that you think is expected of you by others.

You alone have the responsibility for *your* actions and reactions. No one makes you respond in a particular way; *you* choose your response. To say "*You* made me angry" or "It's *your* fault" is to deny responsibility for your own responses. If you cannot admit to any complicity in a conflict you may only perpetuate it.

But, you say, don't I have a right to be angry with:

- The husband who walked out on me after ten years of marriage?
- My boyfriend who was unfaithful with my best friend?
- The boss who criticized me unjustly and fired me?
- The sexist attitude of my colleagues (clients, boss, customers) who call me "honey" or "dear" instead of by name as they do my male counterparts?
- The kids who don't pick up after themselves, wash a dish or respond when I call?
- The department store that doesn't make the delivery on the appointed day when I've taken time off to be there for the delivery?

We are sure you can think of hundreds of situations, from merely annoying to seriously threatening, that give rise to anger. In each you would feel fully justified in seeking revenge or making the other party pay. The skilled negotiator, however, will pause before blowing her stack, during which time she will assess her own role, and review the facts, her objectives, and the possibilities for making gains or minimizing losses for both sides. If she does decide to express her anger, it will be a conscious act and not simply the kind of explosion that contributes to a deteriorating situation.

Taking Risks

Many women avoid negotiation because they are afraid to take the risks it will involve. Much more than men, they take rejection as a personal affront.

Accepting Rejection

"When you want something, go back and go back and go back, and don't take 'no' for an answer. And when rejection comes, don't take it personally. It goes with the territory. Expose yourself to as much humiliation as you can bear. Then go home, and do it all again tomorrow."*

This advice must be internalized by any would-be actress who pounds the pavement and knocks on doors looking for an opportunity. She knows all about risk and rejection and has learned not to personalize it. Indeed, she expects it. Everybody in her position is suffering the same temporary fate. It is more in the nature of a ritual, a rite of initiation, and easier to endure because her self-esteem doesn't rise or fall with each blow. Taking risks in a negotiation may not as often subject you to rejection, but when it does the sense of humiliation may be greater. However, learning to take risks is essential to becoming a skilled negotiator.

Remember, a negotiation is any situation in which two people meet with the intention of changing a relationship. Any effort to affect a change in the status quo involves risk. If one party is too timid to attempt it, it's not a negotiation but an acquiescence. Just think—if, for example, you are afraid to risk asking your boss for a raise, or to risk telling an errant child that you want her to reevaluate a plan of action, you are automatically the loser. But the other side will likely lose too because the animosity your failure generates in *you* will make future negotiations with the other person more difficult. When we refuse to take a risk, we must contend with the self-critic in each of us that recognizes we've abdicated an opportunity. In the long run, this is a greater

---

*Betty Furness, speaking at a conference at Marymount College, in "Advice to Women at Midlife," *New York Times*, February 7, 1983.

punishment because the failure of courage compounds, making it increasingly difficult to take the next risk.

Although learning to take risks is a high priority, it needs patience. It's very hard to do and there are many setbacks in store. Each time you do it you will have to rev up your courage anew. Only after a good bit of experience will you get to the point where the terror abates.

Facing Your Fear

What is the fear? Looking stupid? Being ashamed? This shouldn't be so bothersome, but most of us underestimate our successes and judge ourselves more harshly than the world does. What a pity! To expect perfection is to fall prey to our own brand of "oughts."

I remember one woman who, in all the time I knew her, never expressed a viewpoint. She was thoroughly agreeable but it was difficult to get a conversation going. The darn thing of it was that she was a very smart woman. I don't know what her past conditioning had been, to result in such passive behavior. I always felt particularly outspoken when I was with her, but only by comparison. She never dared to express a point of view in opposition to her husband, and my guess is that his pressure on her was so overwhelming that she gave up her right to negotiate. This learned behavior of playing it safe, never expressing a contrary viewpoint for which she could be held accountable, became the way she protected herself. Thus, I felt that she missed the subtle shadings of relationships, the give and take, the mountains and valleys that make people interesting to each other.

Taking Action

"Take back the power you have given others to inhibit you with a questioning look, a curt dismissal, or an uninformed challenge. Act on your right to express your thoughts and feelings. No one gives you the right. It is yours to exercise. Change your quiet and cautious image by speaking up. Others will respect you for taking risks and will welcome your involvement."*

Have you noticed how some people with obviously limited

---

*Celia Halas and Roberta Matteson, *I've Done So Well, Why Do I Feel So Bad?* (New York: Macmillan Publishing Co., 1978.)

ability succeed and have no qualms about sailing into any new situation? They take risks as if they were wearing protective shields that allow them to run a hazardous course and emerge unscathed. But for most of us, the first step—recognizing and accepting our lack of self-confidence—can be a boon! Admit it to yourself—you're a sufferer in this league! At least you won't have to pretend to yourself, knowing that you tend to undervalue your efforts and need to self-correct constantly. A little risk taking is in order.

Sometimes you seem to be taking a risk because someone else perceives your action as daring and dangerous. Forbidding a hostile and burly hospital attendant from moving my sister from a bed to a stretcher when she had a possible broken back (it was, indeed, broken) I never gave a thought to the wrath I might incur. He was furious at my interference but I stood my ground and the whole bed was wheeled to X ray. There was nothing frightening to me about asserting myself in this instance, so I didn't perceive the situation as holding any risk. Other people felt I had acted courageously in the face of his abusive reaction and admired the risk I took.

On the other hand, speaking before a large group of people was, for years, too great a risk for me to take. I feared it so much that once at a local branch of the League of Women Voters, when I had to make a report consisting of no more than a column of figures, I fainted on the spot. I avoided public speaking for most of my life, until one day I made a conscious decision to take the plunge. I was asked to prepare a seminar for delivery a year hence: How long did you say? A year? Sure. The glib response, the quick decision. The half-jesting acceptance of something I knew would traumatize me! And it did! Having agonized for months before the actual event, I felt like a zombie that first time. But in retrospect I think agreeing to it was the result of a negotiation with myself to overcome a bugaboo once and for all. By putting myself in the position of burning my bridges, so to speak, I forced myself to confront the fear. You can see how decision making and risk taking go hand in hand.

Conquering this fear was not the result of just one episode but of many speaking engagements that followed, and was the single most significant negotiating aid I developed. I learned that one *can* get over big stumbling blocks. All sorts of benefits resulted. I found my voice and now I am not afraid to use it. The effect is freedom—to speak or not speak, plan my moves, develop dialogues, not worry about the event in which an opinion is asked of me. Since I am no longer afraid of having to speak, I am better able to observe and listen during a negotiation. I can more readily seek information, intuit needs, plan strategy, keep control of my end of the proceeding—that's power of the most potent kind!

Risk Is Inescapable

Implicit in risk is the concept of change. Even if we don't choose to take a risk, time, itself, changes everything. A loved one becomes ill; parents age; a child goes off to school; finances necessitate that you work for a lifetime, not just for that stopgap period you had foreseen; good fortune projects you to a new social plateau. Even changes for the better can feel risky.

Risks imposed from the outside are even more taxing than those we've consciously chosen to undertake, because they are usually negative, take us by surprise, and produce feelings of helplessness. Why should a husband leaving for another woman, a loss of job, or a move to another country be called a risk? Because each of them implies change; finding new means to implement a change forced upon us by painful circumstances is the risk factor.

Recognize that change—even for the better—is stressful, and risk invites change. Also recognize that avoiding change is not only stressful but more damaging because we can't escape that self-critic in each of us.

A First Step

If you are hesitant in taking risks, and if this hesitancy is a cause for concern because you feel you're shortchanging yourself, then something needs to be done. However, you don't become a risk taker simply by making the decision to be one.

The next step is not to throw caution to the wind, but to find a risk you can take with *some* chance of success.

Try some small risks at first:

- Express your feelings more freely.
- When someone offends you, have the courage to let them know how you feel.

- Risk the embarrassment you fear in making a long overdue apology.
- Break out of habitual molds. If your business reports follow a specific pattern, try a different approach; add graphs, pictures, interviews, etc., so that your new format will gain more attention.
- Try an exercise in mild outrageousness.
- Join a committee that puts you in the limelight.
- Tell a joke even if you're not a jokester.
- Call someone you think will reject you.
- If you are generally withdrawn, try to speak out.
- Experiment. Behave in a way neither you nor others expect you to behave—and judge the effect.

A friend decided to take this last type of risk after we discussed her problem of getting attention from salespeople. She had the feeling, whether justified or not, that they ignored her, but the fear of further rejection made her reluctant to speak up. It's a relief once you own up to a fear because you don't have to punish yourself for the feeling any longer. That frees you to take the risk of doing something about it. She consciously decided to act in a fashion dramatically opposed to her normal approach. I wish I could have been there to see the scene. She gathered her courage, put on her most imperious manner, and, with a posture to match, strode into the fur department (no less) and spoke her lines. "My good man, I want to see your latest fashions in mink. My time is limited so I'm going to seat myself here on this sofa. Please bring them to me immediately!" And so he did, in great haste, and with the proper deference to a prospective customer.

Taking this one risk opened a new world of possibilities. Although she's not planning to play out that particular scene again, she *has* learned that there are many ways to negotiate getting attention, and she won't be afraid to use them. She didn't buy the mink coat, but she had a lovely afternoon.

The Value of Anxiety

Don't run away from anxiety. It's normal to feel it when anything important is at stake, and it actually helps you by focusing your energy and attention.

An actor said, "I used to be afraid of my anxiety. Now I know how much it does for me, how much it enforces concentration and energizes my work. So when I start feeling anxious, I hail anxiety as a friend. Hi there, anxiety, old pal. What can you do for me today?"

Making Decisions

Closely allied to taking a risk is making a decision. Being blocked in one creates a problem in the other. Because women are so often afraid to take risks, they lose the opportunity to make decisions and lack of practice only compounds the fear of both. It is a self-perpetuating paralysis, the cure for which is in the doing. You cannot negotiate without taking risks and making decisions, and women need to practice both these skills.

The Hurdles

TRUSTING YOUR OWN VIEWPOINT

Before you can take the risk of expressing your viewpoint, you must make a decision as to what it is. Deciding what *you* want and how *you* feel is the first step. This does not mean you should make hasty decisions just to avoid looking indecisive. Educated decisions result from true evaluations of situations. The problem arises when you tentatively develop a viewpoint but refuse to put yourself on the line for fear of whatever repercussions you dread:

- *They* might not approve.
- I will be punished.
- I'm afraid to take the responsibility.
- I'm afraid I'll be wrong.

Although you may be able to hide the fact that you avoid making decisions, you can never really fool yourself. *You* know it's insecurity that prevents you from having a definite viewpoint. But why the panic? After all, you don't have to stick to it if someone convinces you that another conclusion is preferable.

Recognizing that you have a problem in this area is the first step toward doing something about it.

FEAR OF MAKING MISTAKES

In order to be able to make decisions you've got to permit yourself to make mistakes. Expect to make mistakes and you won't be deterred from making further decisions because your last one was wrong. Decisions must be made and you cannot expect always to make the best one. For one thing, there is usually no "best."

By the time we make a decision, the circumstances leading to it have probably changed. By the time you implement it, a different set of circumstances already exists. Even if you examine the situation minutely, hoping to line up solid criteria as a basis for a decision, realize that there must be a lot left out in your consideration. Your perception is always selective and can never encompass everything. So you can never be sure you are making the best decision.

Helpful Hints

However, there are methods of evaluation that will aid in decision making.

CULTURAL BIAS

It is important to remember that we see everything through the filter of our own culture, religion and experience, from which we derive our biases. If two people see the same event there is little likelihood that their perceptions of what they have observed are identical because each has abstracted from the event those "facts" most pertinent to him. This should comfort us if we realize that the decisions people make are not based on indisputable fact. All is perception. When we understand this principle we do not berate another for a decision inconsistent with our thinking, nor do we blame ourselves for holding a different view. Rather, we try to examine both sides with an eye to arriving at a view that both can accept. That's what we hope happens in the negotiation process.

TIME FRAME

Everything that happens to us occurs in a specific historical time which necessarily colors that experience. Thus your experience as a child in 1940 would be different from the experience of a child today. If, as a young adult, you fell in love in 1960 your experience would have been different than your daughter's would be today.

Not considering this would make it very difficult to describe and explain this experience to your daughter.

INDEXING

Indexing assists in straight thinking. Consider politician 1, politician 2 and politician 3. The classification "politician" tells us that they have something in common, while the index number reminds us of the individual differences between 1, 2 and 3 that have been left out. Remembering to index will catch us up short when we make a statement like "business is business" (a rationalization for ignoring the ethics of a situation), or "kids are irresponsible these days" (a blanket indictment ignoring completely the unique attributes of individuals), or "men are all alike" (a pronouncement that fortifies a prejudice and precludes seeking better relationships).

CHECKING THE TERRITORY

Little of what we know is a result of direct observation. Our knowledge comes to us in large part through speaking to people, reading books and newspapers, radio, TV and schooling.

We must recognize that the verbal world (which includes the words we read) and the actual world stand in relation to each other as a map does to the territory it represents. In making a decision one should try to get closer to reality by checking the map against the territory. This enables you to better assemble the facts. Crossing a street when the light is green without looking right or left is a simple response to a signal. Checking the territory—i.e., looking—can help avoid an oncoming bicycle traveling at such speed that the rider can't possibly stop.

The ancient Greeks believed that a woman had less teeth than a man. This knowledge was derived from a system of logic which concluded that since her mouth was smaller it couldn't accommodate as many teeth. Unfortunately, nobody bothered to count them. Had they done so we would have known earlier that both sexes are equal, at least as far as teeth go.

HABITS

One high-level female executive has told me that her method of making decisions (which she never agonized over) is to clear off her desk each day by making every decision required of her and leaving nothing for the next day's consideration. This has become her habit, and it allows her to start each day without the encumbrance of yesterday's problems.

If making a decision is not easy for you, it probably causes stress in even minor daily aspects of your life. Planning in advance and providing yourself with lists of alternatives can save you time and energy.

• Plan clothes for a week, and accessorize at the same time.

• Have a list of restaurant recommendations on tap from critics and friends.

- Make files of leisure activities to pursue.
- Use recommendations of others wherever possible to help you make decisions. An ingenious friend of mine introduced me to his system of evaluating recommendations. He would always keep the source of the recommendation on file. If, after acting on a person's suggestion, he found that it proved unsatisfactory three times, no further consideration was given to that source and it was stricken from his list.

You may find that the habits you establish for making minor decisions carry over into the more important ones. In any case, they will free you to concentrate on the decisions that are harder to make.

How to Make a Good Decision

In decision making we seek to limit our risk by:
- fact finding;
- recognizing assumptions and hidden assumptions;
- seeking additional points of view;
- changing levels.

You live in New York and you've been offered a job in Denver which will mean moving your family and starting a new life, and will require your spouse to change employment or agree to a commuting marriage. In short, your decision will have profound consequences and will require a negotiation with yourself as well as with others.

Your *fact finding* may reveal that the increased salary is substantial enough to support the family while your husband seeks reemployment. You must now question some of the other aspects involved. Will your children make a good adjustment? In the back of your mind do you see your future in New York and this move as a temporary one (a hidden *assumption* you've unearthed)? Has your husband really examined his feelings about the move? Would *you* be happy with a weekend marriage if he chose to continue his job in the East? What *additional points of view* have you sought? How do the grandparents feel about the family moving so far away? What other jobs closer to home might offer more incentives? Which is a higher priority for you—your career or the life you've built at home? Have you thought of *changing levels*? One aspect that might affect your decision is that if you assume breadwinner status, the emotional relationship between you and your husband will need renegotiating. Only after very careful consideration of everyone's needs will you feel secure in arriving at a decision.

You may need some schematic aids to help you arrive at a decision. Consider these:

- Draw up a balance sheet listing the pros, neutrals and cons as a means of clarifying your thoughts.
- Analyze your short- and long-range goals. Then analyze your wants and musts and compare each goal to your wants and musts.
- Set a deadline for decision. If you can't make a decision by that time that may be an act of decision itself!
- Sometimes just flipping a coin can end the dilemma, although not in a situation with as many complications as changing your life and the life of family members.

How to Avoid Making a Bad Decision

What are some of the factors that lead one to make a "bad" decision?

Prejudice prevents us from seeing each situation anew. In the 1960's young people said, "You can't trust anyone over thirty," and it became the rationale for a way of life. On the other hand, labeling college students as unpatriotic because they demonstrated against the war in Vietnam led to a mentality in which the Kent State massacre could occur.

Friends of mine who were treated superciliously in Paris restaurants and found Parisians unwilling to understand their French have translated that experience to all things French, making the "bad" decision not to visit "that country" again. All of us have prejudices. Let's try to recognize them and retest our assumptions. Otherwise we'll be making bad decisions without realizing the prejudicial basis from which the decision stems.

Reacting emotionally and too hastily to a situation carries a big risk of making a poor decision that a delayed reaction might have negated or modified. If we allow ourselves to be pressured by a powerful antagonist, or by someone who is attempting to intimidate or flatter us, we are playing into his hands, and not allowing ourselves to assess the territory sufficiently.

Sometimes we make a decision because it's expected. As part of a group we may be reluctant to stand out like a sore thumb and so we go along with a consensus point of view because we think we need the support of the group. That support may no longer be needed or wanted, however, if we decide, after the fact, that the decision was immoral.

If you believe it's all right to take advantage of another person when the odds are stacked in your favor, you may look back later on *that* decision as a bad one, if only because the other party will retaliate in some way, at some time. You haven't laid the groundwork for a good working relationship. If, on the other hand, you base your decisions on the long-range criteria of the better good for *all* parties involved, they'll be more successful and you'll build more credibility. People will have more confidence in your powers of judgment.

Decisions and Negotiating

Above all, decisions, once taken, must not be considered as carved in stone. Decision making is part of a process world. The ability to make decisions must not preclude flexibility in a negotiation. As feedback and new facts emerge, goals and positions may change, necessitating altered decisions.

People who make decisions, whether they be business or personal, are willing to assume responsibility. When asked what determines the actual decision, a word often mentioned is intuition. The years of experience leading to intuition, the data, the gut feeling—whatever you want to call it—is the accumulated wisdom earned from "doing it."

Decision making is a skill that needs to be used if it is to flower.

Communication

A willingness to talk to each other is of course an essential part of every negotiation and, in general, the more open and explicit you can be, the easier it is to arrive at solutions. This does not mean that anything and everything should be aired in all situations. Women are generally more willing than men to be open about their feelings, and so they can often focus on the sources of personal conflict more readily. However, a woman may be *too* sensitive. She may be more concerned with how she feels than with the substance of the issues, and this may hamper how she addresses both business and personal negotiations. If the other party in a business meeting attacks her position, she may take it personally and, instead of focusing on objectives, she may communicate only her anger. Conversely, because she is sensitive to other people's feelings, she may expect others to respond to her emotional needs without being asked. If her feelings are hurt, she may cut off meaningful communication. Consider those circumstances when you choose not to speak. For instance:

The Perils of Silence

Someone is unjust to you, but you don't acknowledge the injustice. You suffer in silence. The other party is not aware of your attitude, even though you're not as cordial as you had been. The objectionable behavior continues and you feel it's intentional. This becomes a way of life until, last straw—no more—you explode!

Results? Who knows! But how did this situation evolve in the first place?

- You set up an illusion of the way someone should respond to you.
- You are disillusioned when the behavior doesn't meet expectations, indeed appears insensitive.
- Your inability to negotiate with yourself and clarify how you actually feel keeps you locked into this unrewarding give and take. The cost is great. You have become a victim, not only of the situation but of yourself as well. In refusing to take steps to remedy an impossible bind, you have acquiesced.

Thus, when the pent-up anger explodes, it is often over an insignificant event.

Keeping Communication Channels Open

Maybe the great drama could have been avoided by posting signs along the way that issues needed airing and that you were feeling bad. Even if the behavior you object to didn't change thereafter, at least you would have put yourself on record. With your feelings known, the parameters of the whole situation could change.

Now don't think that communicating feelings is license to go in there fighting! If you do, expect a fight in return! Your aim is to establish a climate that works for you and your movements should be in that direction.

- Keep passion in control.
- Actively seek to ascertain the other's needs.
- Mentally put yourself in the shoes of the other person seeking to develop understanding and empathy.
- Don't be discouraged if things don't change right away.
- Be persistent in your quest to establish a positive climate.
- Even when you're at the receiving end of a hostile or thoughtless climate, respond in a positive fashion.
- Be deliberate in this endeavor. Your purpose is to get that negotiation back on track, on a firm footing, and ultimately to satisfy your objectives.
- Remember that our facial expressions, the gestures we use, and the attention we give to listening are important aspects of the messages we communicate. Sometimes the words we speak and the gestures accompanying the words are incongruent. If one has to choose between the two messages, the overwhelming tendency is to believe the nonverbals, because they mirror feelings more accurately.

Taking Responsibility

If keeping communication channels open is so critical for the fruitful continuation of a negotiation, what prevents people from taking steps to achieve just that?

One of the stumbling blocks is fear of exposure—revealing too much of oneself, being chastised, rejected, demeaned, or losing power. We've spent years developing the defenses that bolster the persona we project. We take a risk in revealing ourselves.

There is also a risk that while we may be raising issues in order to encourage some mutual understanding the other party may interpret what we say as challenging, disapproving, disloyal or downright hostile.

Well, is it? Is our attempt at communication merely that outburst of pent-up anger? Are we expressing our feelings in terms that another person can accept?

"We ought to look not only at the disagreement but also at the mood in which it was expressed. When someone disagreed in the inquiring mood, the other fellow was often encouraged to make efforts at accommodation. But let the note of suspiciousness or dismissal sound and overt hostility was its echo."*

Are we being direct or manipulative? This is truly a moment for self-examination, for uncovering assumptions and assessing needs—theirs as well as ours. It can also serve as a sharp reminder of our objectives, and of the desirability of a positive climate.

Why does the onus fall on us? Why do *we* carry the responsibility for "making things nice"? Isn't this just more of the same nurturing trap that women are prone to?

Yes! No! Maybe! It depends on your point of view.

Yes, if you're too embittered and angry to be objective, then you may interpret an accommodation or any positive effort on your part as sinking into a hole you've been down before.

No, if you keep coming back to your objectives, one of which is to keep the negotiation perking. You will use any means from nurturing to brick throwing to do just that! You will try to establish communication by deliberate action and you will avoid the larger trap of *reacting* to the stimulus you've been offered. You *can* be true to yourself and your values and still keep your hostility under wraps.

Maybe there's a little of both taking place! But so what? What's your purpose in all this? To communicate, enlarge the pie, create new dimensions upon which you can build. To start a new regime—one that encourages a more honest give and take so the festering can't get started.

Ground Rules for Expressing Feelings

Certain ways of expressing feelings are acceptable and others are not. The more negative emotion we bring to a situation, the greater the danger of a failure in communication. We may express a great deal of anger to a salesperson who has been rude, but the effect of that expression and the success or lack of it in resolving the ~saction is not as significant or long-lasting as the effects of ngry exchange with a loved one. So, the extent of involvement w..n people is important in assessing the effects of airing one's feelings.

*Irving J. Lee, *How to Talk with People* (International Society for General Semantics), p. 48.

For instance, I returned an item to a department store and was met with an impermeable wall of rejection. I didn't have the sales slip. There was no way of knowing when the item was purchased and nothing could be done! I was infuriated, as I lost no time in conveying. Although blowing off steam did feel good for the moment, it in no way altered the circumstances. I still had the merchandise and I still wanted to unload it. At such times, it's wise to remember that no only means what one allows it to mean. It certainly needn't be believed. In fact, it is always a challenge that should make one ask, why not. In some instances no may remain no but if you don't investigate the why not you'll never know whether you could have prevailed. Upon my changing levels, the manager of the department found it easy to resolve my dilemma and also proved adept at smoothing ruffled feathers. Whether true or not, I had a sense, as I left, that new guidelines for treating customers would be forthcoming.

When ongoing relationships need to be negotiated and re-negotiated frequently, the stakes are higher, the difficulties greater, and the perils more substantive. The need for communication of the sort that heals is essential, since you are not dealing with a single transaction, but with a series of ongoing events in which the atmosphere in each contributes to the resolution of the next.

It may sometimes seem easier to avoid dealing with confrontational issues. You may think that if you use the strategy of forbearance, time itself will bridge the gap and the issue magically disappear. Unfortunately, emotions are not so compliant; while the surface may be smoothed over, the underlying issues will resurface at another time, reinforced by resentment. Better to learn ways of expressing your feelings initially, without destroying the negotiation.

The first step in the process is to get in touch with your own reality; know what you're feeling and how strongly. You're out for the evening with your husband and he makes a disparaging comment about your talkativeness. To be sure, it's couched in amusing terms, but it doesn't sit right with you. Why? Try to recognize what you're feeling. Is it anger? Embarrassment? Humiliation? The moment passes. The evening proceeds well enough and the feeling you registered is muted for the time being. But it still rankles, and you feel you must talk about it. How do you do it without provoking an argument?

The short-form map is particularly helpful here.

- What are your objectives? What do you hope to achieve in this negotiation? If it is to heal and to better your relationship, you'll speak in words calculated to do that. If it is to punish, to make the other suffer, go back to square one—that's war, not negotiation.
- What do you need and what needs can you ascribe to the other party? Do you want an assurance of love? Is it your self-esteem that needs bolstering? Can you see the need of your opposite number to save face and be similarly assured?
- What climate will you create? Will it be a positive one in which further communication will be tolerated, and do you understand that this is a prerequisite to a successful outcome?

Getting Others to Talk

It's important to listen to everything, even what is not being said. If your secretary gives you the silent treatment, it's a communication. If questions to your child about where she's going and what she's doing yield the replies "Out" and "Nothing," you know you're on different frequencies. How can you handle the silent treatment? That depends on the degree of your interest in establishing rapport. If this is indeed your desire, pursue it—show the interest that the silent one hopes to elicit from you. A cautionary note: If you ask for explanations, be prepared to endure the onslaught that may be forthcoming before things can be righted.

Rose de Wolf has some suggestions that are helpful in getting someone to speak to you.*

- Ask questions that require more than a yes or no. Asking how the meeting was is not as effective as asking who was at the meeting and what was the main topic discussed.
- Tell your story first. You're likely to get more of a response than you would if you put someone on the spot by expecting them to relate a tale to you.
- Talk about a subject of interest to both of you.
- Be a good listener. Listening, attentively, is a stimulus to conversation.
- Acknowledge conversation. Respond appreciatively if some-

---

*"Speak to Me, Baby," *Ladies Home Journal*, September 1983.

thing nice is offered. "It makes me feel good when you notice the effort I put into that report."
- If someone does open up to you, never make that person sorry by using that information for attack in a subsequent argument. A betrayal of trust will not be forgiven.

Remember that your silence can be a blessing, too. If somebody has done something stupid, he knows it and doesn't need a reminder.

Some Communication Killers

Alfred Fleishman pinpoints some ways to sabotage communication in a business situation.*
- *Interruption.* Before the other person has a chance to finish a thought, interrupt and provide the clincher to his argument.
- *Diversion.* Change the subject to steal the other person's thunder or draw attention away from him.
- *Name-calling.* After his argument is put forth, tell him he's off his rocker or he's got to be kidding.
- *Challenge the speaker's integrity.* After the full presentation, instill doubt with such questions as "What's in this for you?" and "What are you trying to hide?"
- *Contradiction.* Say authoritatively at the close of his presentation, "You're wrong!" If he defends himself, shrug your shoulders and repeat it without being drawn into an argument.
- *Laugh it off.* The whole thing is so ridiculous, you imply, that only your good nature keeps you at the meeting.
- *The brush-off.* An expert can make someone feel so insignificant that he retreats.

If you want to sabotage business communication, these tactics will assure your spoiler status.

Beware the Truth

Don't think that telling "the truth" is the answer to the communication problem either. How we communicate the truth and the moment we choose to share it has as much to do with how it will be accepted as does its validity and our intent in revealing it.

*"How to Sabotage a Meeting," *ETC: A Review of General Semantics*, vol. 24, no. 3, pp. 341–44.

Truth can sometimes mean merely sharing excessively painful data with another person to relieve a burden of guilt. Some people mistakenly feel that the truth will magically solve problems. Telling the truth requires discretion rather than indiscriminate blurting. Gerard Nierenberg and Henry Calero's book *Meta-Talk* contains this warning: When someone says, "I'm going to be perfectly frank," expect an assault.

Silence, rather than the revelation of truth, can be a compassionate act. Acknowledgments of indiscretion are better left unspoken.

Honesty is a difficult game with no hard and fast rules. When asked for your honest opinion, ask yourself:

• What is the relationship and is it secure enough for a genuine answer? What is the climate at the time the request is made?

• Is the person asking for truth while in a state of anxiety? In that case, you need to be sensitive in giving your answer.

• Am I feeling hostile? Will I respond in a you-asked-for-it-and-I'm-going-to-give-it-to-you mode in an effort to use the "truth" to hurt?

• Will I be telling the truth as I see it for their good or for my own?

• Is this the time for truth? If my friend is ready to go out on a date and asks how she looks, what purpose will be served by saying "lousy" or "I've seen you look better"? The greater priority is her self-confidence, which might be shattered by your subjective truth. Anyway, that's not what she's after in asking for it.

Conflicting Expectations

Communication between intimates is a negotiation that goes on forever and requires all the effort you can give it. All too often, it breaks down or dwindles to a trickle, occurring only at the most superficial levels: "Did you get the mail?" "What's for dinner?" "You were supposed to call the plumber."

Studies suggest that women are more tuned in to the emotional content of life than are men, and more eager to explore these lines conversationally. The camaraderie between men is generally of a sort that doesn't delve into the emotional realm whereas women appreciate the empathy and understanding derived from conversations with other women. And they listen with more attention and patience than men are willing to devote to this area of communication.

It boils down to needs and expectations. If a woman wishes for a male companion with whom to share her feelings, she must assume the responsibility for trying the techniques we've mentioned. If she remembers that an ongoing negotiation is in progress, she'll be focusing on an exploration of needs and the ways of fulfilling her objectives.

Sometimes her needs and his will be at odds. What good the recognition if the dichotomy exists? To fulfill the needs of another is no pleasure if you're denying your own! In such a situation, you'll avoid being too disheartened if you remember that needs are constantly changing. The most taciturn of companions who has life by the tail today and communicates only in the most pragmatic terms to satisfy his needs may tomorrow seek your attention to express doubts, fears or even joys—in effect, what he's feeling. Such moments are very nice indeed when they occur.

You cannot expect another person to fulfill all your needs for emotional satisfaction. Respect the other's way of being and keep the climate positive to maximize possibilities.

The Tough Ones

In a relationship turned difficult, be absolutely clear about your motives before uttering words you know will wound. If you don't make a great effort to set things to rights, the words you've spoken will assume undue significance. Communicating bad vibes without a subsequent healing alters the shape of a relationship—for the worse. But maybe you intend to gradually wind down a relationship through a series of slow deaths, thinking to lessen the blow when the end finally comes. Each person must seek his own path in such a delicate matter. This is a negotiation of the most subtle kind. Examine your objectives carefully, examine your needs and the needs of the other, don't get locked into positions, and, most important of all, restore a positive climate. It's not easy but it's not impossible either. It will take effort, more than you might imagine.

If you are dealing, at this point, with a hostile party, be realistic. Don't expect magic just because you're negotiating in good faith. You're getting flak, you've said the right things, and you didn't turn your antagonist around. You're no longer in the realm of negotiation proper but mired in emotional content. Don't let yourself be drawn into such a battle. Just as it's best to deal with the angry, explosive, hot-tempered boss by contributing your comments after his tirade has run down, don't now get drawn into a rebuttal. Perhaps your tendency, due to uncertainty and frustration, is to keep quiet, contribute nothing, wait and hope it will blow over. Instead of relying on the tactic of forbearance, waiting it out, or any other strategy, keep lines of communication open; be a contributor, make the effort—the ball is in your court. Silence will be interpreted as a gesture of dismissal, a pointedly hostile act, even though you may be using it for lack of knowing what else to do to avoid further unhappiness. This is the time for lightening the mood; humor, affirmations, connections and recognition of joint interests are all helpful.

And if in the final analysis you judge this as a negotiation that failed all is not lost. Anything you have contributed to an effort to restore balance will accrue well to you, even if the deal fell through and the parties separated. The animosity will lessen with time and the parties can meet on another occasion knowing that the chances for other negotiations between them is a distinct possibility.

Getting Your Point of View Across

Many people, both men and women, either fear to speak, don't choose to put themselves on the line, or simply don't have a strong viewpoint that they wish to expound. Gender is, for the most part, not the important factor. On the other hand, women may be more reluctant to speak up or draw attention to themselves in the belief that it's not acceptable female behavior to be too assertive—an assumption that may be fortified if, indeed, they are ignored.

We've so often heard it said by women who serve on boards of companies or philanthropic organizations: If a woman makes a suggestion it is automatically ignored or turned down on the spot, only to reappear as a gem of wisdom from the mouth of some man. There must be some truth to this, for it comes up over and over at seminars where women express grievances. One very prominent woman on the board of a hospital spoke to this issue at the meeting I attended and confirmed it as a fact she constantly had to cope with. "It's incredible, the devices I use to get my point across," she said. "Just today I took a fellow board member out to lunch and had to plant the idea in his ear! Manipulative, you say? You bet! But I'll resort to manipulation to get an important idea on the table. Sure enough, in this afternoon's session, he proposed my idea as if it were his own! I don't mind that as long as he carried the vote. As I suspected, it was accepted quickly, as it never would have been if I had made the motion."

But women needn't resort to this oft-used device of enlisting a male confederate to act as spokesman to get their ideas on the table. Using the techniques of negotiation, women are perfectly capable of speaking up themselves.

In a Meeting

How should a woman negotiate at a meeting to maximize her potential and downplay the disadvantages—real or imagined— of being female?

• *Pay attention to the way you present yourself.* Especially in your nonverbal presentation, your aim should be to project self-confidence (whether you feel it or not). First impressions are not the whole picture but they set the tone. Creating a good image does not entail making yourself so visible through a contrivance that everybody takes note of your presence. A sensitive, relaxing aura will more readily convey the confidence you want people to feel. Tone of voice, an open countenance and a friendly demeanor will lay the groundwork for your contribution to the meeting.

• *Place yourself strategically.* If seating is not preordained, you have an opportunity to place yourself in the forefront, preferably alongside someone of prominence, certainly not clustered in a group of women. Prior homework will have informed you of the composition of the board, and within bounds of propriety you may be able to place yourself advantageously.

• *Study the agenda* so any remarks you make will be presented at the proper time. In discussions with your colleagues prior to the meeting, you will gain some information on important issues that are not stated in the formal agenda. Knowledge of the inner workings will be helpful in maintaining the good impression you've made initially.

- If you are part of a team, try to *clarify your position* and learn what function you're expected to fulfill. That will keep you from making inappropriate remarks at the wrong time. When you do speak, you will have the force of team approval to legitimize your words.
- *Use questions skillfully* to gain attention as well as to gain information. Be aware that questions can be perceived as a threat and make an opposite party defensive. Frame them in such a way as to avoid engendering antagonism.
- *Try to make personal contact with fellow board members.* Over the course of your meetings you can add to your list of business friends and you will be acknowledged by a widening group of people—a big status builder. If you don't make the effort to get to know people you retain an anonymous status, and you won't get the attention conferred by friendship when you speak.
- *Be succinct and to the point.* If you practice economy in your presentation of ideas, they will more likely be favorably received.
- *State your ideas in a clear, confident voice*, as declarative statements. Women have been accused of sounding tentative and overly polite. Avoid tag phrases like "don't you think?" "if you wouldn't mind," and "is it all right?"
- *Consider the price to be paid for volunteering* for a special assignment or participation in a committee project. Do you have the time to honor such a commitment? Is it worth the rewards to be gained (status, visibility, a chance to speak up next time)?
- *Always keep in mind your objectives, the needs of the group, and the climate you wish to create.* If you're having trouble presenting your views, planning a strategy may provide you with a framework from which to consider alternative tactics and how they may or may not help:

Is it wise to forbear or would it be better to speak out? Can you enhance your position by association or will you be seen as self-serving? Should you use fait accompli or will you be challenged on it? Should you change levels, an option to pursue if you're stuck? Should you ask strategic questions, and have you considered the effect?

Don't get hooked on any one tactic; flexibility is more important. Any tactic or strategy can be countered when it is recognized. It is more productive to make genuine contact with the people you're dealing with and respond to their needs and the needs of the business itself.

Remember that you have a valued point of view to contribute. Having learned how to negotiate, you are competent to present it.

The Use of Questions

The skillful use of questions can be a valuable tool if you are looking for information.

On the other hand, their tactless use can create a barrier to negotiations. Anyone sensitive to body language will recognize when someone feels threatened by a question—the look of surprise or fear, the body tensing, possibly followed by an angry retort. At that point, the direction of the negotiation may veer out of control as the issues raised by the unfortunate question are pursued.

In formal negotiations, questions should be prepared in advance with an eye to the function that each one will perform. We will show how different types of questions help to move the negotiation along in a smooth and orderly fashion.

In interpersonal relations of an ongoing nature or a brief encounter, what may or may not be considered a permissible question is as variable as the cultures of the party, their sexes, the length and nature of their relationships, and the tacit boundaries set up by the parties. For example, the questions you might ask your daughter concerning her current beau might not be permissible to ask your stepdaughter if you have not established a very close relationship.

Before asking questions in interpersonal relationships, examine your own need to know against the needs of the party you are questioning (these needs are generally of esteem, love and belonging). Of utmost importance in such relationships is maintaining a climate that encourages the continuation of communication.

One thing you may have to be prepared for when you ask a question is an unexpected response which changes the parameters of the negotiation. You are annoyed at something your best friend did and ask her why she did it. She responds with such a tirade that you realize she has been harboring strong resentment against you. Your response will now depend upon your own needs in the relationship and may demand that you call upon many other negotiating skills such as flexibility, creativity and attention to the climate.

If you don't understand an answer to your question, ask for clarification. The person who is answering may be deliberately vague to see whether you are paying attention. It is bad enough to misunderstand when you think you understand—it's worse not to try to understand at all.

The Question Map

In a business negotiation skillful use of questions can secure immediate attention, maintain interest in the matter under discussion, and direct the course you want the negotiation to take. The use of questions is a powerful negotiating tool that must be employed with discretion and judgment.

The question map below can assist you in this. With this map before you, you can prepare your negotiation in advance. You will notice that Function III questions, those which create a negative or hostile climate, are missing from this question map because we think they have no place in a negotiation. Knowing what you plan to ask in advance gives you an opportunity to move question by question to a close. It also gives you an opportunity

QUESTION MAP

Start _____ Finish

Function 1 Questions (To gain attention)	Function II Questions (To get information)	Function IV Questions (To stimulate thought)	Function V Questions (To close the deal)
1. _____	1. _____	1. _____	1. _____
2. _____	2. _____	2. _____	2. _____
3. _____	3. _____	3. _____	3. _____

Function III Questions not used
(because they damage the climate)

to listen more attentively to what the other person is saying without having to consider what your next question should be.

The Five Functions of Questions

Questions function in five ways to help or hinder your negotiation efforts.

FUNCTION I: GAIN THE OTHER PERSON'S ATTENTION:

Hello, how are you?

How is your family?

How is your golf (tennis, handball) today?

May I ... ?

Would you be so kind ... ?

These openers serve as attention getters. Some cultures demand that a great deal of time be spent on these opening questions, which are part of the amenities exchanged between the parties.

Part of the preparation for the negotiations should include research on the background of the parties so these opening questions can be relevant to them. Also relevant would be any background information on how they handle such questions and whether they should be kept to a minimum.

FUNCTION II: GET INFORMATION:

How much does it cost?

When will it be delivered?

When is the next scheduled train?

All these are designed to get information on data which are or can be readily made available. Ordinarily, such questions do not produce anxiety in the listener unless the reason for wanting the information cannot be ascertained.

FUNCTION III: GIVE A NEGATIVE MESSAGE:

Very often questions are designed to give information rather than to receive it. Consider for a moment the role of the receptionist in your office. Someone telephones your office and asks for you. Your receptionist asks who is calling. The caller gives his name and is placed on hold while you are asked whether you are in to the person making the call. If you decide not to take the call, your receptionist announces that you are not in. The effect of that exchange lets the caller know that you are in but do not wish to speak with him. This information will lead the caller to feel anger or resentment. Another example of giving information with a question can be observed in the technique of a manager who looks at his watch and asks an employee who arrives late, "What time is it?" That question notifies the employee that the manager has witnessed the late arrival and is noting the time.

In interpersonal relationships, questions of this nature can appear to be an attack upon one's esteem needs. For example: A friend relating various health problems with which she was recently beset was met with the question, "Are you a hypochondriac?" If this question was taken to be a reflection of what the questioner thought of her friend's problem, there might be a serious breakdown of further communication between them. However, given a long history of friendship and serious concern, the listener might respond to that question as if it were a fourth-function question.

FUNCTION IV: START PEOPLE THINKING:
This form of questioning puts your thoughts in another person's mind.

Have you ever considered . . . ?

To what extent . . . ?

This form of questioning can stimulate creative thinking, such as, if we utilize such and such material, what kind of product would we get?

It can be helpful when you are negotiating with a representative of a company who must report to higher authority to ask the questions she is likely to get from her boss, so she will have time to think through the answers.

Getting back to the question posed of the possible hypochondriac in Function III, the friend might examine her symptoms in the light of that question. Of course, anxiety can be a byproduct of such a question, unless it is perfectly clear that her esteem needs have not been endangered.

FUNCTION V: BRING NEGOTIATIONS TO A CLOSE:
Knowing when a negotiation is ready to close and how to do it is a skill. You might recognize without much difficulty that you've made a sale of your widgets when your prospective purchaser asks whether they come in purple or when he can have delivery. Asking when he would like delivery can bring a negotiation to a close. This kind of question needs a good sense of timing since it can cause anxiety if you try to lead the listener to where he may not want to go.

If you want to put an end to a friend's overly long monologue for which you do not have another moment to spare, you might interrupt by asking, "Why don't we meet for lunch sometime to discuss this further?" This question, accompanied by your body movement toward the door, should signal a close.

Nonverbal Communication

Reading nonverbal behavior is an art that gives you insight into the nuances of communication and allows you to read what's really going on, regardless of the words being spoken. When you are trying to sort out all the input you are getting at a negotiation, it is perhaps the most significant method of evaluation. You learn when your arguments are on target, whether you're being received hospitably, whether your opposite number finds you believable, when things have gone sour, or when you've arrived at a point of agreement sufficient to get a signature on that dotted line.

The importance attached to reading nonverbal behavior is a relatively recent phenomenon, dating probably from 1970 when Gerard Nierenberg and Henry Calero wrote *How to Read a Person Like a Book*. Now people-watching has become part of the negotiation process. Several people on a team of negotiators may be assigned the specific task of observing nonverbals of their opposing numbers, and what they see will be discussed at the end of each day with the same seriousness accorded other aspects of the proceedings.

Because women are attuned to feelings, and feelings are often expressed in gestures, many women excel at understanding nonverbal communication. As mothers, women also get an education in this area, because children who do not yet talk provide a veritable laboratory in the meaning of gestures.

Reading Clusters

Someone said to me the other day, "I just can't believe that gestures tell as much as you say they do. I often stand with my arms folded across my chest in what you would call a defensive stance. And it's just not so. I do it because it's comfortable. It's no more than that." I would agree with him that a gesture such as the one he described is not particularly significant, at least not as a single gesture. But suppose that particular way of standing was accompanied by other defensive gestures. Suppose he pushed his chair back, increasing the distance between himself and the person he was talking to. Suppose he turned himself sidewards like a fencer or locked his ankles. Such a cluster of gestures would indeed be a sign that his attitude had changed—and not for the better—in regard to the negotiating relationship. Sequence and clusters of gestures are highly reliable tip-offs.

You may ask how reading clusters helps you recognize what your opponent is feeling and what you can do about it. Such a cluster indicates the extent to which circumstances have changed, and you'd better do something! *Rethink* what's going on. What words did you use preceding the change? Did something threatening take place? Was a lack of respect shown? Did you demand a concession? Had you become defensive yourself and shown nonverbal signs of increasing hostility? Something went awry. The situation has lost its center and needs to regain it before you're back on course. What does the other side need at that moment? Have safety and security been threatened, or have you stepped on his esteem need? If you can decipher the needs, you can correct your error.

Sometimes bizarre gestures accompanied by equally strange or dramatic verbal responses indicate a strategy of surprise—an effort to catch you off base, disorient you, or interrupt your train of thought. This may be an effort to intimidate. While you're trying to sort out in your mind the meaning of the dramatic change, stand your ground. Wait and see, and don't buckle under the pressure.

When you don't yet feel at ease in a situation, you may overreact to the nonverbal feedback you think you're getting. In other words, your own mindset may influence your perception. When I first started speaking to large audiences I reacted to their gestures with anxiety. Audiences are neutral and expectant when they first greet a speaker. From the podium, if one lacks confidence, this can be interpreted as unfriendliness. During the speech all shades of interest and disinterest emanate from an audience. The speaker must be careful not to be overly influenced by them. She has the responsibility to be well prepared, organized, and to deliver her message as best she can. Don't expect a sea of friendly faces and you won't be chagrined at the reactions you get. They're normal.

The Ambiance

Nonverbal cues also come from the settings you find yourself in. Who is sitting at the head of the table? Who's to the right of the grandfather? Who has the nerve to interrupt others? Surely this person holds a position of authority if the interruption goes unchallenged. Some people in authority who revel in their positions will literally place their chairs on a higher plane so they can look down at those who come before them. Executives who wish to create a hospitable setting often design a living room atmosphere in their offices, such as chairs around a cocktail table, in which people can talk more convivially and with ranking deemphasized. Certainly this kind of climate is immediately more cordial.

On the other hand, a negotiator with a winner obsession will resort to any device to gain a point. He may seat his antagonist with the sun shining directly into his eyes. He may even offer a chair with shorter front legs that keeps the occupant sliding uncomfortably forward. Nonverbal dirty tricks.

A good manager gets the pulse of the office by observing nonverbal behavior. Ethel noticed a change in Donna's routine. Her personal phone calls increased and she took more care with her grooming. These were the first intimations of something new going on. Her lunch hours were longer and she adopted a very relaxed attitude about completing work. A request to push up vacation time was the final tip-off that she planned to quit. It did not come as a surprise.

By reading others skillfully a manager can forestall problems and improve productivity.

If Marge's finger goes to the side of her nose when you ask her to type an extra report, that's her gesture for doubting she can do it, but she doesn't have the guts to say no. Check further to see if you can break the job into parts that she can readily handle.

If Vera doesn't know the answer to the question you asked, her gestures are defensive and she becomes particularly quiet. You need to explain the reason for your question to allay the fears it provoked in her.

If normally gregarious Joe is silent, is the sadness you perceive a result of a situation at work? Your empathy will be appreciated.

Reading Your Own

Even more significant than reading nonverbal behavior in others is the fine-tuned ability to read your own. If you find yourself walking dejectedly with a hangdog expression, feel it, question it, and delve into the reasons. That way, you can self-correct. You can more easily maintain the image you wish to project if you can monitor the outward manifestation of your feelings. What does the pitch of my voice, the tilt of my head, or my facial expression reveal? What did I do that made my opponent fold her arms across her chest or cross her legs in the opposite direction and tilt her body away from me? Why did her voice suddenly elevate and change from a pleasant to an angry tone? Don't try to change the gesture by itself, but think it through and try to find the source. Then the change becomes easy.

It would be wonderful to have video tapes made of ourselves in the negotiating process, but since this is not always possible, the next best thing is to take mental snapshots of ourselves periodically during a negotiation. What am I doing with my face, my hands, my legs and my body at this minute? You might be brought to an abrupt halt by the realization of what your nonverbal communications are revealing despite all your verbal disclaimers or reassurances.

If you know that gestures tell how you feel, can you learn to inhibit those signs that are a dead giveaway? It's possible, but not too likely! So why try to do so? Better to understand how you're feeling and deal with *that*. Richard Nixon would have been better served if he had not tried to orchestrate his gestures for specific effect. He seemed out of sync, and therefore insincere. After the Watergate debacle, he became much more relaxed and, as a consequence, more believable. Only a consummate actor, like Ronald Reagan, can use nonverbals effectively to create a convincing characterization.

Expressions

Women engage in nonverbal communication not so much with broad body movements as with facial expressions and inadvertent hands. Tightly clasped hands may indicate anxiety. If she brings her hand to her throat, or pinches the skin of her hands, a woman may be saying, "Is this really me in this tight spot? What do I do now?" (Just remember that you cannot interpret any single gesture without seeing it in a context.)

The face tells many stories. A passive poker face is nonetheless gesturing—the intense effort not to display emotion must be hiding something. Facial muscles give clues to states of tension or relaxation. A smile with clenched teeth does not seem friendly, whereas a natural smile creates an atmosphere of relaxation. A finger to the nose usually means doubt or indecision. Eyes flash in anger, dance with pleasure or are veiled. If someone's eyes wander excessively as you speak, make an effort to get attention. Her mind is elsewhere or else she's avoiding your direct gaze for reasons you need to fathom. If it's difficult to read a face, the negotiation may be more taxing than you had supposed.

There may be cultural and personality differences to take into account. The British tend to maintain longer eye contact and shake their heads as if in agreement as you make each point, but this merely means that they heard you and are respectfully waiting their turn to respond—or retaliate. Some people are naturally charming and expressive; this does not guarantee a short, easy negotiation.

Reading nonverbal behavior is only one tool in the negotiating process. You still need the whole preparation process to understand the people involved and assess the situation accurately.

Recognizing Meta-Talk

The Meaning Behind the Words

What we say is the largest part of a negotiation. However, behind our words are layers of meaning that complicate the process.

We can identify at least three levels of meaning:
• what the speaker is saying;
• what the speaker thinks he's saying;
• what the listener thinks the speaker is saying.

The word Nierenberg coined to describe the meanings behind the words is "meta-talk." These meta-talk speech patterns are often roadblocks in any relationship or negotiation. They obscure and confuse communication because they send out contradictory signals which may or may not be understood. It is unfortunate that most of us, both men and women, generally ignore these signals. Insight into meta-talk enables us to understand underlying needs, our own as well as those of others, and this understanding can facilitate the negotiation process. While to understand another person's meaning accurately may not remove difficulties, and may indeed exacerbate them, at least you know where you're at and that's a beginning.

So much of what we say is not an attempt to communicate but to obscure a meaning, circumvent a conversation that seems too risky, or protect ourselves in a veil of platitudes. We seek, above all, to protect ourselves. We resort to insinuation rather than say something directly particularly when some things are better left unsaid. A case in point is the remark one woman made to another at a luncheon: "Was your husband out with his sister last night?" The recipient of such a remark may well perceive the hidden message, but that knowledge doesn't undo the damage.

If I catch myself saying "honestly" or "I want to be perfectly frank" I'm embarrassed because I know the effects these words have when they're used on me—I am immediately suspicious and my antennae go up. Yet the user feels like he's made a point.

When I hear "by the way," I'm cued into the fact that something significant will follow, although the speaker strives to give the opposite impression.

Some negotiators try to intimidate you: "Don't you even know that?" If you are properly intimidated you may answer with your own variety of meta-talk rather than risk saying, "No, I really don't. Would you tell me about it?"

I am wary when someone says, "Yes, I was wrong, but..." That verbal eraser—but—is a way of rationalizing a false statement or explaining it away at my expense.

Some questions—Do you really like the dress? Do you think the boss liked my ideas?—are not requests for your opinion but pleas for affirmation or empathy.

A whole category of meta-talk falls under the heading of downers:
- Are you happy now?
- Don't make me laugh!
- Don't be ridiculous!
- Needless to say.

The intent in such derisive statements is to make you doubt

your own competence. You don't have to be victimized by such manipulation if you recognize the purpose of the meta-talk. You don't have to rise to the bait.

The odd thing about meta-talk is that people who use it don't realize how transparent they are. Some people are so eager to identify themselves with success that they think they can horn in on credit that other people have earned. They use "we" to try to lead people to believe that they are part of an inner circle, when, in actuality, they are on the periphery.

Name dropping falls into the same category. It is a thinly disguised effort to make people believe you hobnob with the great, near great, talented, affluent or desirable. It's not communicating with someone but a message you're delivering to your listener in an effort to get acceptance and admiration. Reflected glory is never sweet. For that reason alone it's a foolish maneuver.

We often denigrate ourselves as a way of seeking approval: "Oh, anyone could have done it; it was nothing." What are you seeking? An affirmation that your act was splendid, worthwhile or significant. If you hear these words, or similar ones spoken, can you provide the reassurance that is called for?

The words we use and the way in which we use them often reflect our attitudes. We separate ourselves from "them" in our conversations, thus placing ourselves on some higher plane and creating the rationale for isolating others from being joint participants: *They* can't be trusted, you wouldn't want *them* in your group, *they'll* never learn, *they're* bleeding hearts.

The greatest benefit in reading nonverbal behavior is the ability to recognize your own gestures so as to better understand the effect you are having on people. The same can be said for meta-talk. The conversational innuendos that we use to get a point across need evaluation. Become skilled at analyzing your own patterns of speech. Self-negotiate to find out what you really want to say, and, if possible, find a way to be direct.

"I have something important to talk about but I won't discuss it now," I found myself saying to my husband. I recognized the meta-talk immediately. What I really wanted was to convey displeasure and create suspense and anxiety. "Look, I'm angry at something. Let's talk," would have been more honest. I said it and we got to the heart of the matter without letting it smolder.

"Let me sleep on it," I said to a colleague when he presented a business idea. I didn't want to come out directly with a lukewarm reaction to the proposal. But he knew what I meant and nothing was gained by the delay. I vowed not to meta-talk him next time but have the courage to be direct. It's not so difficult to eliminate meta-talk once you recognize what you really want to say.

Meta-talk is an evasion, whether we wish to think so or not. To catch it in ourselves, as well as to recognize it in others, gives us one more negotiating skill.

Self-Assurance

Self-assurance is an image women have only recently begun to cultivate. Many women still feel that it is more natural to blend into the background. This hampers their negotiations. Don't count on getting that promotion because you're decorative, cheerful or competent. It doesn't work that way. If you haven't made your ambition known, you're just as likely to be passed over. Here are some tips to avoid getting left in the bullpen.

If You've Got It, Flaunt It

- Speak up! Let it be known that you're ambitious.
- Get involved in committees.
- Take courses.
- Develop a new competence. (Learn a language if your firm is international.)
- Expand your social contacts and include the higher-ups if you can.
- Don't eat lunch with your friends each day. This is an excellent time to make new contacts.
- Send a reminder to your boss if you've been promised a salary review.
- Keep a running list of your accomplishments. Leave nothing to memory when review time arrives.
- Want to travel? Make it known that you're available. Management assumes that women don't choose this option.
- If opportunity knocks, grab it. Don't let your fears stand in the way and don't let the moment pass.

• Ask for an opportunity—on the basis of your credentials and ambition.
• If the answer is No, keep yourself visible. You've made yourself known, and another chance will come up.

If You Don't Have It, Flaunt It Anyway

It is to your advantage to appear self-assured whether you are or not. If you don't seem so, you're not believable, and you won't be taken seriously. You can train yourself to convey this image. People want to deal with someone who inspires confidence. It's not deceitful to present your best face and it makes good sense. Even if it's painful, make the effort.

Don't cancel your positive image by expressing self-doubt. It doesn't matter if you feel anyone could have done it. The fact is, you did it and you should reap the rewards.

Discuss self-doubts with a higher-up? Better not! Even if he views you as competent, a wedge of doubt will enter his mind. He will begin to watch for validation of your self-denigrating view. You don't want that. Even if you lack assurance because of your inexperience, do your best and keep learning. As you do, your doubts will fall by the wayside.

Scripting an upcoming event can help you prepare for it. How will you start? When will you introduce a point? Suppose she says she can't buy your point of view? What will be your answer? Are you ready with facts? Have you prepared the questions that will give you insight into her needs? If you are fearful of how your words will come across, rehearse before a live confederate, not necessarily for a critique, but to get the feeling of a real audience. Often, that's the hurdle that needs to be bridged and to do so prior to the negotiation itself can reduce some apprehension.

What's the worst that can happen? After you've pinpointed as many dire consequences as you can imagine, they may not seem so bad.

Chuck Reaves explains that in order to get one yes you may have to hear twenty no's. He called this the theory of twenty-one and it is just such persistence that overcomes obstacles.* There

*Chuck Reaves, *The Theory of 21* (New York: M. Evans and Co., 1983).

are always people who say it can't be done, it shouldn't be done, or it won't be done. Those who don't succumb to negative thinking and who refuse to give up are the ones who keep seeking alternative solutions in a negotiation. They go that extra distance and make things work. In a negotiation, the self-confident spirit is infectious and sets the climate for a good resolution.

Betty Furness, in "Advice to Women at Midlife," says women should never take no for an answer and should fake only one thing: confidence. "If you don't have confidence, lie in your approach. No one wants to know if you're scared. It makes them scared, too. Be absolutely sure of yourself, and, if you're not, fake it."*

It's a good challenge. If we're lucky, we constantly find ourselves in new situations with no previous experience to draw on. We are stretched and enriched by such encounters no matter how stressful the experience. A few times in the arena and you will learn to wear that confident attitude as comfortably as a pair of jeans.

Admittedly, it's antithetical to say, on the one hand, be forthright and learn to express your feelings openly, and suggest on the other hand that you always present a confident aura, even when you don't feel it. However, the time to express self-doubt is before or after a negotiation. Then it might do some good. Avoid an abject confession of ignorance during a negotiation.

Putting across a feeling of confidence even when you don't feel it requires taking the risk of not carrying it off. So what? Ask yourself what's the worst that can happen if you try. Your inner voice might retort: "I won't convince them. They'll see through me. They'll know how I feel anyway and I'll seem like a fool; or, worse, I'll be ignored and I'm back to Square One, only feeling even lousier." It's at this point that you need to persist. How will I feel if I don't try acting confident? I'll probably not make the impact I would, not get to say what I want to, my effectiveness will be curtailed. But the worst of it is, I'll hate myself in the morning.

---

*The New York Times, February 7, 1983.

Knowing Value and Price

Women often feel handicapped in a negotiation because they don't know how to assess what they're being told. One area in which this is often true is knowing what things are really worth.

Lack of savvy about value can make any negotiator feel inadequate. Therefore it's important to assess the territory as much as possible beforehand. Costs are sometimes defined in actual terms, such as money or material value, but can also be assessed in terms of convenience or inconvenience, the time spent on a transaction, reliability of source, the need to make a decision despite cost, or other factors—some of which may impel you to make a deal that might, initially, seem out of line costwise. Price is a nebulous term and is constantly changing. Knowing whether it is rising or falling is part of the process of recognizing value.

Some people are more skilled than others at making quick determinations of worth, usually because they have experience. When buying a couch one may be guided by a quick look at the size, the material, what similar ones cost, the uniqueness of style, the function intended, the budget allowed for the purchase, delivery time, guarantees, the discount possibilities, and so on. (And all this mental calculation done in a twinkling.)

Whether you're buying an item, hiring a workman, dabbling in real estate, dealing with a supplier, or asking for a raise, you should know the worth of what you're dealing in to fortify yourself against making a bad deal. If something is too expensive, you'll need to try to bring the price into line or restructure many other considerations. If someone offers you a service at a price much lower than competitors offer, beware of hidden costs or unreliability. If you're seeking a raise, know what your job function is worth on the market; also calculate how much it will cost your employer to replace you.

All of this involves doing homework. Check comparable prices, reputation, past reliability and recommendations.

Negotiating a Bargain

There's nothing wrong with attempting to bargain. In most parts of the world it's expected. It would be laughable for an American tourist to pay the asking price at a Far Eastern bazaar. In addition, customs of many countries demand conversational amenities of a formal nature before a deal can be concluded. Sensitivity to the mores of the milieu in which you're dealing is no more than courtesy, and ignoring this aspect of the negotiation may set a hostile climate.

Sometimes a seller needs you more than you need the item in question. He may be stuck with a large inventory, have a serious cash flow problem, or even be desperate for a sale in order to survive yet another week. What a chance to set your own terms! It's tempting to resort to strategies and tactics that will further reduce the price, but beware of going too far. I was witness to such a negotiation in an antique store in New York that was selling out its entire stock because of the need to vacate within two weeks. A customer was interested in purchasing a large piece of Oriental pottery. She and the proprietor had arrived at a price, one that was lower by far than his asking price. But the buyer kept asking for one small additional concession after another. As I witnessed the proceedings, I guessed that the owner really needed the money because he was conciliatory. But as each agreed-upon reduction became the basis for yet another demand, I could observe the owner's frustration mounting until finally he let go of his Oriental "cool," asked the customer to leave, and said under no circumstances would he sell the pottery to her—*at any price*! Here was a classic example of how the I-win-you-lose mentality can make a deal fall apart. So irritated was the proprietor that his hostility spilled over to me, the next customer, and it took me several minutes to persuade him that our dealings would be distinctly different in character from the last episode.

Many times it's really difficult to know the worth of something. Whether the price is fair or high may be secondary to your wanting it anyway. But you can still negotiate, even in such an illustrious establishment as Harrod's in London. This elegant and imposing department store, known the world over, seems an unlikely locale to strike a negotiating bargain. Yet here's what happened in one instance, which I know to be true because I was the negotiator.

I went to Harrod's to buy a set of Wedgwood dishes. In line with the theory that we're all negotiating all the time, I began by asking a pertinent question. "I know that Wedgwood is price-fixed. Why is it that some stores in London offer different prices for some Wedgwood sets?" Without batting an eye, the saleswoman responded, "Oh, those are discontinued lines." I asked, "What is that?" She said, "If Wedgwood doesn't intend to keep a line in stock for the next seventy years they classify it as a discontinued line." I asked if she had any of these lines in stock; she pointed them out. I was able to buy enough at the discounted price to allow for any breakage that might occur over the next seventy years.

The unknown in this case was whether there was room for negotiation. Without trying I never would have known. Setting the climate was the critical factor; that and the conviction that the situation was negotiable.

Perhaps the success with the Wedgwood china gave me heart in attempting another negotiation. Although bargaining is a standard and expected procedure in Hong Kong, I was warned that the Communist Department Store was one place in which the stated price was absolutely firm. And so, when I had found there some bracelets that I loved, I didn't even think of a traditional negotiation in which I would ask for a price reduction. What did go through my mind was the possibility of altering the terms. My question to the young woman behind the counter must have been a first, for she surely didn't have the answer. But she agreed to consult her superior. I had said, "Those are lovely bracelets. What is your quantity discount?" After a discussion with her superior she came back to announce, "The quantity discount is ten percent!" I said, "In that case, I'll take these three bracelets."

The Good-Guess Factor

Occasionally a circumstance occurs in which you presume value and price are compatible, and an immediate decision is called for, not allowing you the time to check further. The apartment I live in is a case in point.

I found an apartment that I liked, but I couldn't make the decision alone. It was too expensive, I had only seen four others, I still had my house to sell, it was all too fast—but, on the other hand, what a view! That Chrysler building was a jewel in the sky. And a garden on top of the world. No matter that the kitchen was falling apart. And who thought to see whether there were any closets! My husband *had* to see this one and he came shortly and not too eagerly in response to my urgent bidding!

He took a look around, agreed that "it looks nice," and after a quick time-out to check the seriousness of my intent said un-hesitatingly those few words that clinched the deal—"We'll take it." Astonishment on my part! Who does such things? No one. How did we know it was worth it? Shouldn't we see some more? Couldn't we get one for less? But buy it we did. And live in it we do. And there aren't enough closets! But the Chrysler Building is lit up at night—it's lovely.

Was this a negotiation? Most assuredly it was. The most important element, however, was the need for a quick decision since it was now or never. Other people were already there with their brokers and the apartment was certain to be sold—that day! Under these circumstances my husband shrewdly judged that negotiating the price or terms was not a possibility. Instead, we were negotiating to get the owner's commitment. We agreed to their asking price on the spot, she called her husband to ver-ify his agreement to the sale, and we had a deal! Afterward, other people offered more to get it, $10,000–20,000 more, but both sides had verbally agreed, and the owners honored their moral commitment.

I wouldn't have had the guts to make this decision alone and I'm grateful that my husband's educated and quick decision mak-ing came into play. What gave him the courage to do it? A shrewd knowledge that time was of the essence, a talent for knowing value (even without the preferred investigation), and confidence in his own judgment! I learned a lot from that. A lesson about the perils of being indecisive and the crippling effects of pro-crastination. I still don't know whether I would now have the guts to buy it that quickly, but I might.

Some hints:
• Know the worth.
• Don't get stuck in bottom-line thinking.
• Get information to help in decision making.
• Make a decision—yes or no.
• If you make a mistake, it's generally not the end of the world.

Intuition

You have now armed yourself for a negotiation with an under-standing of the facts and assumptions. But there is another element you must not forget: Intuition, that elusive phenomenon, is so difficult to analyze but it can clue you in to the subtleties that make or break a deal. When is the proper time to disclose what you *really* want? How do you know when the other side has made its final offer? Is your boss's open door really open to you at a particular moment? Is it the right time to approach your friend about the delicate situation that bothers you? How can you strike the proper balance between expressing your needs and listening to the other party? When is time about to run out?

You can't add up a column of figures or read a report to give you the answers to questions like these.

Women and Intuition

Intuition is no longer the stepchild of the thinking process. When it was referred to as women's intuition and was attributed solely to the female sex, it flew in the face of male reliance on logical thinking and thus was downgraded. Women were suspected of being incapable of reason. To explain those instances when they came to sound conclusions and offered valuable thoughts, the myth grew that women's intuition was the explanation.

The importance a woman attaches to personal relationships leads her to observe human behavior with keen attention. What she learns this way translates into intuition. The process can be likened to an educated guess, a notion, a hunch, an intimation. The more information we gather, the more acutely we observe, the better our intuition. As we learn to use our intuition more often, we become more successful at it, or, put another way, we are right more often. Sometimes it's a mixed blessing. The many minute signs that we've been registering in our brain computer may result in a momentary flash: He's screwing around. I just know it! Often the intuition proves accurate!

Don't think, however, that intuition is an infallible process. A woman in court waiting to be interrogated for jury duty raised her hand and the judge asked her to speak up. "I can't serve on this jury, judge!" To his request for a reason, she answered as she pointed a finger accusingly, "One look at the defendant and I just know he's guilty." The judge replied, "Sit down, madam, you're pointing at the district attorney!"

Intuition is the end product of half-conscious but innumerable minute observations. Attention to detail, keen observation and a caring mentality are traits women developed to deal with other people. It was a matter of survival. Now they are using it to further their careers as well.

However, not all women benefit from the skill and many men have keen intuitive powers and are proud of it. In the area of negotiation, such a sensitivity allows one to see the subtleties that lie beneath the surface of the spoken words and the strategies employed. It enables you to recognize and respond to the underlying needs of your opposite party and that may ultimately be as important as the substance in providing a basis for agreement.

If You're Not Born with It, You Can Learn It

Make an effort to sharpen this skill as you strengthen your arsenal of negotiating aids.

- Consciously observe people for detail.
- Attend to gestures and particularly look for patterns in gesture clusters. You can intuit the right moment to put a pen in the other person's hands for the signing of a satisfactory agreement.
- Note the meta-talk behind the spoken words, and attitudes and meanings below the surface will come clear.
- Ferret out the facts and assumptions. The more data you've unearthed the better your intuition will be.
- Jot down ideas (that ever-present pad and pencil is imperative). They often hit you at odd moments, only to be lost if not written down. A tape recorder is a handy device for quick notation.
- Learn to act on your hunches, in small-risk situations at first. You will gain confidence in your decision making if your intuitive feelings have been part of the process.

Intuition comes in a flash, as opposed to data gathering. Maybe after all the measurable aspects of a situation have been considered, a final decision is based as much on a gut feeling as on the facts themselves. Have you been using phrases like: I have a feeling, my hunch is, off the top of my head? Your intuition is coming to the forefront.

Warren Bennes, a professor of organizational psychology and management, spoke to top leaders and found that his subjects paid little attention to textbook theories and management styles. They tended to trust their hunches more. They also seemed unaware of the possibility of failure, an attribute Bennes calls the "Wallenda factor." According to Karl Wallenda's widow, the famed aerialist never thought about the possibility of falling from a high wire during a circus performance. Once he began to consider the possibility, he plunged to his death within a few months.

Intuition has one enormous advantage. It impels one to act. Don't expect it to be infallible. But since there is no certainty to an outcome no matter how many facts can be assembled, one's gut feeling may be as accurate a barometer of the accumulated data as you will get.

FIVE

Barriers to Negotiating with Others

Negotiation is a give and take. As such, it involves interplay between or among individuals. It is therefore also subject to whims, habits, prejudices and personality traits of the particular humans taking part, including ourselves. And these individual characteristics can be helpful or harmful to the outcome.

Part of your skill as a negotiator is to recognize those aspects of behavior, your own as well as that of others, which throw up roadblocks and inhibit the possibilities for a win/win resolution or indeed sometimes any viable solution at all.

In what follows we describe a number of such patterns and how they can be countered.

Power

At every seminar that we give for women, we are asked to address ourselves to the concept of power. We are asked how you get it, how you wield it, or how you contend in the face of it.

Perhaps the first question to ask is what power is. Broadly speaking, one can say that power is the ability to influence people in order to achieve those things you want or think should be done.

Unfortunately, people generally think of power as the ability to tell other people what to do. But it's more subtle and complicated than that. Telling people what to do doesn't in itself ensure its getting done (as most of us know). Getting people to do what they don't want to do is an exertion of power over them, and it can sometimes work temporarily and even for long periods of time, as in authoritarian states, families in which one person dictates the rules, or offices in which bosses tyrannize their employees. But when power is used in this way, it can actually get in the way of achieving one's ends—for the one exerting the power as well as the one oppressed by it. When power is perceived as force it naturally elicits anger, resentment, frustration and/or rebellion.

The negotiator with an I-win-you-lose philosophy should expect a reversal of her fortunes. Her opponent's energies will be devoted to making her lose, sooner or later.

The ability to persuade others that your purposes are the same and the ends you are trying to achieve are in everyone's best interest is a more effective use of power.

One of the most powerful men I ever knew defied every common conception of how a powerful man should look or behave. Marty, a lawyer, was large and awkward. He carried his hulking body as if it were painful to him. He wore his clothes wrinkled and his hair unruly and he had a perpetual hangdog look. He was soft-spoken and gentle, almost diffident with clients, staff and advocates. He was not afraid to say, "I don't know," and he encouraged his staff to research thoroughly before they proposed solutions to problems. If a mistake was made, his chiding was gentle. He never muscled or demeaned anyone. He never harassed or demanded, but he was never refused or resented, whether the request was for a cup of coffee or overtime. The willingness of his staff to work beyond the call of duty was legend and his ability to attract clients enabled him to build a large, prestigious law firm. His power resulted from his brilliance, his understanding of other people's needs, and his ability to create a climate which enabled others to be responsive to his needs.

Unfortunately, the Martys of the world are rare, and we are often faced with an exercise of power that makes us feel victimized. The thing to remember in any negotiation is that you may have more power than you realize. There are many *sources* of power apart from position and authority: one's talents, intelligence, knowledge, character, charm, stamina, health, patience, ad infinitum. And there are many *kinds* of power other than making people jump to your demands: knowing what you can and can't achieve; standing your ground in the face of anger;

making decisions; knowing when to quit; creating a supportive climate. This power is available to anyone who wishes to exercise it. The questions to ask yourself are: What power do I have and am I using it in the best interest of this negotiation? What power does the other party have, and how can I counter any unproductive aspects of the way he is using it? Even when starting from a perceived position of little power, the use of negotiating skills can affect the ratio.

For example, an administrative assistant who feels indispensable asks her boss for a raise. If, because she feels he cannot run the office without her, she immediately threatens to leave if not given what she wants, her threat may rouse so much antagonism that he acts against his own best interest in firing her. She can better achieve her ends by presenting him with the validity of her need for a raise and listening carefully to his reaction, even if negative. If she makes him realize that she understands his needs and problems—e.g., his inability to pay her more, or his need to feel that she is loyal to him or interested in the welfare of the company as well as in the money—he will probably be more receptive to working out a mutually satisfactory resolution. On the other hand, if he is unwilling to respond in any productive fashion, her most powerful counter may be to look for another job before she quits.

How many times in the course of a seminar has an attendee suggested, "But don't you have to hit the opposition on the head to show him your potential?" When we turn it around and ask whether *she* would like to be hit on the head, the invariable answer is no. Look at negotiation not as a contest of power, but as the opportunity to be supportive and positive in creating solutions and resolutions that will be kept by all sides.

Intense Emotions

Women are often accused of being too emotional, and it is probably true that, when provoked, we are quick to respond emotionally.

While it is good to express how you feel, the problem is how and when. In the throes of an emotional upheaval, one does things one may regret at a later time. Anger dictates lashing out, getting back at, telling the "truth," righteously setting things straight, seeking retribution, wanting to win. But there is no winner in such a flare-up. Too much self-esteem is invested by both sides, and in calmer moments we can see that it is better to prevent a fight from going that far.

Negotiating techniques provide a method for coping with a situation that otherwise might end in a loss for both sides.

Don't become the victim of an emotional obsession. You can recognize the symptom—so much energy focused on a situation or person, that it dominates your thoughts. This is very difficult to combat, because in the throes of such emotions you rake up the past, dwell on supposed injustices, and feel totally victimized, whereas a calm examination would undoubtedly reveal a contribution on your part. Worst of all, escalating emotion can initiate action directly contrary to your own best interests. You may fantasize ways of setting things right, meting out justice or taking revenge. You may even make attempts to implement these plans. But you are more likely to assume the role of sniper, taking jabs whenever you can, hopefully delivered at the pressure point most likely to cause discomfort. This is no longer a negotiation—you are starting a war! Are you aware of it?

Negotiating with yourself can point to a better way. Sometimes, though, your automatic method of responding is so strong that you can't easily make a change. The emotional baggage you carry precludes acting in your own interest, indeed stops you from negotiating, even with yourself.

When you're out of control, you need a way to pull yourself back. If you were playing a competitive sport, you'd call time out. Do so now. Take a breather. What *is* this emotion that is consuming you? Identify it! Jealousy? Anger? Guilt? Hostility? Hurt feelings?

For purposes of analysis, attribute a persona to this emotion. What does this emotion want you to do? Strike back? Retaliate? Punish? Embarrass? Hurt?

Where will these actions take you should you pursue them? Try to figure out what satisfaction you might get from acting on your emotional impulse. According to the Sedona Institute in Arizona, there are two factors at the basis of our emotional actions: We are seeking either approval or control. This may be too simplistic for you, but it's nonetheless useful at this point, as a gauge. If your potential actions lean toward the hostile, retaliatory end of human response, it is not likely that you are seeking approval. You are more likely to be seeking control over a situation, but instead of achieving it you will probably encourage a destructive emotional response from your opponent. Escalation is the name of *this* game and the viciousness that can follow is limitless.

When we observe two children engaged in a verbal battle, we rationalize that they're acting like children. Sometimes we intervene hoping to bring reason and ethics into play.

When very old people are crotchety and difficult, we make an excuse: It's because of their age, some alteration in mental capacity. In both cases, we cajole or we distract, we smooth over, we use our influence to restore a reasonable balance. We don't try to make the situation worse by taking sides or introducing inflammatory statements. I attended a wedding and witnessed a situation that illustrates this point. The bride's grandfather was clearly upset. I was close enough to hear the rumblings. He didn't like the table at which he had been seated for dinner; he didn't like the people at the table, the music was too loud, and he was too close to it. The complaints issued forth as each new source of discomfort occurred to him. I could see his anger increasing. At the same time, I could observe the tension building in his son, the father of the bride. I thought an angry exchange was about to erupt. Fortunately, what occurred instead was a good negotiation. Realizing that Grandpa's need for love and esteem were at the basis of his anger, his son called him in front of the gathering to say a prayer and bless the bread. Finding himself the center of attention restored the old man's sense of importance and dissipated whatever discontent he had been feeling.

Instant deescalation! Equilibrium was restored, to everyone's relief. Maturity, not childish vengeance, prevailed.

This was every bit as much a negotiation as if a prospective client reacted emotionally to a presumed slight. One party to the negotiation assessed the territory, uncovered the needs of the other, acted to satisfy them, and created a climate of goodwill. That made cooperation possible—and no one lost in the transaction!

I know from my own experience that the most difficult moment to hurdle is when I am consumed with an emotion that impels me to act precipitously and perhaps counterproductively. That is the instant when I must be wise enough to force a pause!

The next step follows automatically. I review my objectives! What do I want to happen? This, and that, and the other. Now comes that all-important question which I must answer honestly. Is what I'm tempted to do likely to fulfill my objectives or thwart them? Only then do I act. And whatever I decide, at least I've given the consequences a chance to affect my decision.

Such good advice. I must remember to follow it next time my blood boils.

Anger

Emotions cannot be put in neat boxes to be analyzed, corrected and dismissed. They spill over, they intertwine, they emerge in tandem. If they disappear it is only to reappear again on some pretext of their own, to be dealt with anew. They are our friends, for they supply a richness and diversity that makes life vital; and they are also our enemies, a source of suffering, forces that reduce us to inaction and despair. When they control us, we often act in self-destructive ways that defy reason. Anger, one of the most powerful emotions, is a case in point.

An expression of anger is the tip of the iceberg. What lies beneath the surface—the underlying cause—may never appear. It's not even always clear who we're angry at. Is it that other party, the one against whom we're railing, or are our angry words the rationale for deflecting anger away from ourselves? It's a complicated process to decipher emotions and a study of their impact on our lives is better left to psychologists, whose training equips them for a more fruitful analysis. Our purpose is to examine anger against the backdrop of the negotiation process: if and how to display it, how to use it, how to avoid the avalanche that collapses the whole mountain.

One thing is certain. Anger is a serious matter and how we perceive it and handle it has much to do with the path the negotiation will travel.

The manner in which you express anger is often determined by the position you hold in a relationship. If you are a boss you have more freedom of expression than does someone whose salary you pay. If you are the dominant party in a relationship, the one who usually makes decisions, calls the shots, is looked up to,

you likely express your feelings without self-consciousness—
anger as well as other emotions. This is true for women and men
alike. Gender is not the issue.

Reacting to Anger

Male negotiators, however, may make the assumption that women
are more prone to emotional outbursts—that they can be moved
to tears, made to feel insecure, browbeaten by an angry male
display. An angry approach is often a deliberate tactic to achieve
just such an effect. It won't work if a woman won't rise to the
bait, if a cool head prevails, and if she sticks to the issues.

On the other hand, certain kinds of typical male behavior are
likely to make a woman angry rather than tearful:
- condescension;
- bullying;
- treating her as superfluous;
- ignoring her views;
- overprotection and the "pet" treatment;
- passing her over for committee appointments or invitations to
  those meetings that really count.

Handling Your Own Anger

What should a woman do in a negotiation when she is becoming
victimized by her own anger?

I've heard "Let it all hang out, and you won't ruin your
health." And indeed, ulcers, heart conditions, all kinds of stress-
related ailments may result from an effort to inhibit this powerful
emotion. But if holding it in can be a punishment to the body,
conversely, giving vent to it can have a deleterious effect too.
Haven't you seen someone in the throes of anger, red-faced,
tension etched in every line of the face, muscles contracted, all
control lost in the heat generated by such fury?

If we feel anger, then let's recognize the intensity of what
we're feeling. As long as this remains an interior monologue, the
effects on the negotiations are subtle. By inference, the opposite
party may feel that something is amiss, with clarification yet to
come. It is at this stage that we can try to sort out the reasons
for this rush of emotion. Am I displaying annoyance at some
irritating quirk? Was that insulting remark made to hurt me? Did

that domestic fight this morning make me want to lash out at someone else? Come to think of it, have I been generally angry most of the time lately even when a situation doesn't call for it? Do I enjoy seeing the effects of anger? Am I using a burst of anger to achieve a quick effect, even though I'm not really feeling angry? Am I letting someone push my buttons? What's going on?

In personal relationships, sounding off doesn't portend the death knell of the relationship. I can always change my approach, give in, mend fences, wait till tomorrow, make a soothing gesture, or respond to a similar act of generosity by the other party—and the fight is over, equilibrium restored.

But if I am involved in a business negotiation, I must take anger more seriously.

- If I am the angry party, what do I hope to achieve? Will an angry outburst sabotage my objectives?
- If I feel justifiably angry and need to get that on the table, can I state my anger suitably? "I feel angry when I don't get a chance to finish a statement" is preferable to "Stop being rude and let me finish talking before you burst in."
- "Get the hell out of here," perhaps accompanied by a shove, is escalation with the implication of violence. Should such a state of anger threaten, an inner warning system needs to be activated before you erupt. *Stop!* Better to absent yourself for a cooling-down period. Nothing can proceed until the heat is off.
- "You're a liar! What kind of a fool do you take me for, giving me a load of baloney like that?" This personal attack can only put the other party in a defensive position of having to justify an action, in either a rearguard maneuver or a retaliation in kind. "Tell me how you arrived at your figures. I can't agree with the results and I'd like your views," gets the message across without the insult.
- "I wish you'd just keep quiet. You're a pain in the neck! There! I'm glad I've said it." Don't be too happy about your righteous pronouncement. It is not only a catharsis. Expressing your anger has other effects. The person you're communicating with has lost face and will want to reciprocate. Furthermore, it probably adds to your own angry feelings, giving them definition and adding fuel to the fire. Carol Tavris, a social psychologist, says, "Talking out an emotion doesn't reduce it, it rehearses it. People

who are most prone to give vent to their rage get angrier, not less angry."*

- "I'm fed up with these delays. Just sign these papers and no more back talk! Do it now, I say!" This calculated attempt to finalize a deal uses anger as a technique to force quick compliance through intimidation. As such, although clearly expressing anger, it is simply a feinting maneuver. Even if it is successful the party who has been coerced will feel resentment. Unless you have a solid deal, it can yet be overturned.

- "You are asking us to expend money for nonsense! I object and I'm certain I express the view of many people here." This effort to include a wider group in an angry display is an attempted power play in which the anger is a device used as a rallying point. Your assessment of the issues and the mood of the group will determine whether the ploy will succeed.

- Shouting, ranting and raving can so disorient the person at whom it's directed and is such an onslaught that the serious breach it causes can be very difficult to heal. After all, if someone's behavior is so unreliable that displeasure will be expressed in such violent terms, the other person has little stake in trying to reach a more open exchange of views. The risk is too high and there are no discernible long-range benefits as long as the unpredictability continues. Better think of ways to get control of your powerful emotion.

As you can see from the examples above, anger can be genuine or contrived, calculated or spontaneous, successful or a boomerang. As an overt negotiating technique, it is risky. One cannot predict the path that a negotiation will take after an angry exchange has been initiated.

But how should we approach anger? Certainly repressing it, failing to acknowledge the phenomenon, is damaging in the extreme.

According to Dr. Leo Madow, "Suppressing anger is perfectly fine if you do it consciously and for good reason. But repression leads to trouble because the person has no awareness of anger."†

---

*Carol Tavris, *Anger: The Misunderstood Emotion* (New York: Simon and Schuster, 1983).

† Leo Madow, *Anger: How to Recognize and Cope with It* (New York: Scribner's, 1974).

Other symptoms such as depression may emerge in its stead. So the important thing is to recognize and understand our anger. This allows a measure of control so that when and if we say our piece we do so in a way that will not destroy the negotiation. Think of the following:

- *Recognize your anger.* Even if you don't like to express it overtly, clarifying the scope of your anger allows you to make decisions about how to handle it.
- *Identify the cause.* Screaming at your mother when she asks why you haven't called may not express anger toward her at all. Maybe she evoked some guilt in you and rather than confront your anger toward yourself, you lash out at her. Displacing anger is something of which we're all sometimes guilty. It's a relief to call it for what it is. Then, if necessary, amends can be made. "Sorry, Mom, I really didn't mean that," can be a sufficient balm.
- *How important is it?* Is it worth ruining an evening out to berate your partner for being late? Will it benefit you to go over the head of your supervisor to take your anger to a more influential person? Thinking logically about the repercussions of the actions you're tempted to take helps you assess the relative importance of the incident.
- Are you hiding your anger, but constantly making rude asides, and looking for that opening to get in a snide remark? Are you aware of your devices and the demoralizing effect of your "sneaky" actions? *Face up to what you're doing and find a way to deal with anger openly and in a fair way.*

Some Dos and Don'ts

- *Take time out.* Count to ten, or even a hundred. Delay, reflect, defuse.
- *Don't attack or belittle.*
- *Don't sulk.* This will only reinforce your anger without confronting it.
- *Try* (it's hard when you're angry, but try) *to see the other person's point of view.* Sometimes you get a warm glow when it works. My blood was boiling when the man behind the counter at the chicken takeout place was overtly rude. I made the grand gesture (a calculated one, for research purposes): "Boy, you must have had some day! Usually you're so friendly!" He bright-

ened. He acknowledged me. He changed. It was nice for both of us at the moment, and subsequently he remembered me as someone who made contact. I now think of him as more than a nodding acquaintance.

- Hard though it be, *say something humorous* instead of that insult that hovers on the lips. While doing a slow burn at a restaurant after waiting thirty-five minutes for service, my companion received attention after he forced a smile from our waiter by asking, "Any place we can get a hamburger around here while we're waiting for the menus?"

- If you have to, *think your anger to yourself*. Wanting to lash out at a supercilious saleswoman behind the belt counter, I instead repeated to myself that old Yiddish curse, "May all your teeth fall out but one and that one have a cavity!" She didn't know what I was thinking but I felt better and she really did give me some good suggestions after all.

When You're on the Receiving End

What happens when you are not the offender, but the innocent recipient? You're being clobbered from left field and you're at a complete loss. All you know is that you're getting angry, too—and you're about to lash back! Are there reminders for you?

- Reinterpret the situation. When someone displays quick anger and there isn't any discernible reason for the annoyance, maybe she's feeling ill; maybe her manner is naturally abrupt and it's not directed at you. Think, "Maybe it's a bad day for her. There must be some reason otherwise she wouldn't have to act so angry!"

- Don't allow yourself to react. Before you say anything, do a mental checklist: What are my objectives? What's likely to happen if I respond in anger?

- Now, having taken that pause, act moderately. You don't lose anything by not being goaded into the anger game. And you don't display weakness (if that is your worry). Nothing prevents you from expressing your anger at any moment *of your choosing* and for purposes of *restoring balance* to the negotiation. As long as it's not just a reaction, the likelihood of finding a better means is substantial. Ask yourself what this person needs— esteem, safety, quiet reassurance?—and what you can do to restore a positive climate.

- Anger can be handled in different ways. Someone who spews it forth and just as easily heals the rift is not as difficult to deal with as someone whose anger is less volatile but longer lasting. Men are less subtle in displaying displeasure than are women, who are taught to be less overt. On the other hand, in dealing with women, many men feel compelled to act in a gentler fashion and the effort is a strain.
- Size up the territory. If it's your boss foaming at the mouth, don't challenge him. If it's a person you're intimate with, be doubly wary. Don't inflict hurt that builds on hurt. The rift widens too quickly. Face-saving is imperative, theirs as well as yours. You must be willing to let it end—and don't bring it up again! Impossible, you say? No, merely difficult.

While anger can be very destructive it is also an energizer. It galvanizes you to thought and action. Thus, we are not suggesting that you should simply accommodate yourself to others. That is not negotiating—it is acquiescence in a win/lose game, with you the loser. But since a negotiation can be destroyed by the thoughtless expression of anger, as well as by its repression, it is up to you as a skilled negotiator to acknowledge anger, express your own acceptability, and counter other peoples' anger productively.

Rejection

You apply for a job and somebody else gets it. The country club doesn't think you'd fit in, nothing personal, just a matter of policy. The restaurant relegates you to a table near the swinging door of the kitchen, far from the table up front where Paul Newman is sitting with *his* family. Your husband has decided he needs to find himself in Tahiti! As you see, there can be degrees of rejection, but whatever the experience, it is always painful and anything you can do to soften the impact for yourself or others is beneficial.

Coming to terms with what has happened, with your ego intact, makes it easier to put it behind you. But if the rejection makes you feel worthless, then you are hobbled, if not immobilized. This is particularly true in the negotiation process: "This report is all wrong." "I can't ever depend on you to get here on time." "This is hardly the time to ask for a raise."

Such statements are critical, poorly stated and hurtful. A

skilled negotiator would never state criticism in such threatening and nonproductive terms. Nonetheless, you, at the receiving end, perceive these statements as rejection. You feel worthless and summarily dismissed.

The Victim Mentality

If it happens too often, you may begin to expect a repetition around every corner. I once had a beautiful white cocker spaniel who suffered from just such an attitude. Every time he poked his nose out the door he anticipated an attack—and he was right! The poor thing had the mentality of a victim and there were enough bullies around to seek him out. Unfortunately, rejection can make it very difficult to engage in the negotiation process. Some women tend to get gun-shy even when they've been shot down only once or twice. If fear of being rejected is too intense you may be afraid to participate even though you may not admit it to yourself. As part of a team, your fear of rejection may keep you silent, contributing nothing and achieving nothing. Or you may not even get to the scene. That job interview will seem pointless if you rationalize, "It's a lousy job anyway." If in fact your fear of rejection is making you avoid negotiating with others, then it is time to negotiate with yourself. Check your assumptions. Perhaps you interpret feedback in a negative light: "She didn't say hello, she's ignoring me again." If such were a complaint against me, for instance, my assumed coldness could be easily explained to the complaining party. I'm deaf in one ear and couldn't have heard a greeting on my bad side.

Ask yourself today, tomorrow and every day from now on, and in practically every circumstance that calls for action on your part, what assumptions you are making. Asking questions will go a long way toward determining whether your assumptions are valid or should be discarded:

- Was my article rejected because it was poorly written? (Not so—it just didn't fit in with their theme for the next issue.)
- Did I lose that sale because I'm lousy at selling? (Not so—he's just overstocked with size 4 shoes.)
- Will I get hurt in another relationship if my boyfriend took off with another girl and I was devastated? (Do a little self-negotiating. Weigh the pros and cons of shutting yourself off from the possibility of getting hurt again.)

- Was my boss unsatisfied with the research I did? He never mentioned it. (Maybe so, maybe not. Take the risk and ask him for feedback before you feel rejected. Time enough for that if your assumption proves true. Likely it's an oversight rather than the worst interpretation you've chosen to give it.)
- Why did everyone ignore me when I arrived late at the party and didn't know whom to talk to? (Say your own hellos to get the greeting you seek. You may seem so standoffish that you are unapproachable. Or perhaps you are too hasty and the acknowledgment you seek would have been forthcoming, if not instantaneous. Beware of the hidden assumption that unless attention is being paid you, you're being rejected. It can color your entire attitude toward life.)

In every instance above, the "victim" has limited her field of activity. Show me someone who has never risked rejection and I'll show you someone who has never put herself on the line! I'm reminded of the story of Sam, who watched in amazement as another man kissed all the girls who emerged from a movie theater. Sam had to satisfy his curiosity. "Don't you often get your face slapped?" he asked. "Sure," was the joyous reply, "but I get a lot of kisses, too."

Fight That Rejected Feeling

If you risk more, you will get a fair share of rejections—and a fair share of successes. One hopes that the balance will tip toward the positive. But daring, itself, brings its own reward, and once you realize that, rejection no longer looms as a spectre. It is simply a risk that can be handled. Experience is the master teacher. If you self-negotiate to confront your fear of rejection, you will have reason to congratulate yourself. And having thus dealt with your own emotions, you're in a better position to negotiate with others.

So, what can you do about rejection?

- Recognize the feeling as it comes up.
- Check your assumptions before allowing the feeling to take hold.
- Check the territory. What's really happening there and does it really have anything to do with you? Reassess your feeling in the light of new insights you have gained.

Suspicion

When Suspicion Is Justified

I know the importance of establishing a positive climate in a negotiation and I fully accept my responsibility for creating one. Even if the other side is hindering the proceedings by being disagreeable or abusive, the obligation is still mine. However, while trying very hard to set the climate to rights, I am very suspicious of their motives, of their strength, of those hidden ploys that may do me in! And I have every right to be suspicious! I don't know these people and I haven't dealt with them before. I'd be an idiot to plunge right in while we are still testing each other out. Do they really want to buy the house? Is this prospective boss giving me the straight goods about the possibility of advancement on the job? Will the complaint department replace that lemon of a food processor?

I owe it to myself, however, to examine the reasons behind my suspicions to see if they are valid. In some instances they stem from what I perceive as my own disadvantages:

- They'll recognize that I'm new at the game and demolish me.
- They'll perceive my lack of street smarts and clobber me.
- They obviously know more than I do and they'll take advantage of it.

You do not want this kind of suspicion to inhibit your ability to negotiate. This is where your preparation with the aid of the negotiation map can make up for years of experience the other side may have, by giving you the information that will allow you to evaluate positions, needs and strengths, and to intuit the views of the other side.

Thus fortified you can carry through the negotiating knowing that you will be able to judge the point at which your initial suspicion can be relaxed.

Self-Fulfilling Suspicion

Whatever you do, don't indulge in generalized suspicion, which is usually unfounded and unproductive. For instance, let us analyze the following lines of thought: I believe (possibly through past thinking) that they're all out to get me in this harsh world. I react with suspicion at each new encounter without thinking it through or examining my reasons, and even though circumstances change with every new situation.

As a practical matter, they're *not* out to get me at all. With such a mindset, I am making negotiation difficult for both myself and the other side. And while my very attitude precludes and stifles any mutual benefits, the less than satisfactory results reinforce my destructive, suspicious point of view in a predictable never-ending cycle.

A Tale of Suspicion: A Lesson in Self-Negotiation

Hazel manages an office in the entertainment industry with thirteen workers reporting to her. Her success is due to her skill in fulfilling the tasks at hand, her ability to make decisions when necessary, and the effort she expends as evidenced by the long hours she puts in. One reason she has to work overtime is the frequent change in personnel. Someone is always leaving under one pretext or another. When examined closely, this particular problem lies on Hazel's doorstep, for along with her strengths comes a weakness. When something goes wrong, rather than accept any culpability herself, she will invariably blame someone else to get herself off the hook, and a surprised underling will receive the brunt of the boss's wrath. Naturally, resentment seethes and yet another worker leaves.

What would Hazel have to do to allay the justified suspicion of the people she directs? If she were to have the following self-negotiation she would find out what kinds of negotiations she should have with her fellow workers—and possibly even with her boss.

SUBJECT MATTER: WHAT ARE MY PROBLEMS?
- I don't want to lose status.
- Fear of being wrong.
- Fear of boss's anger.
- Underlings should have come through even without my overseeing.
- So they're wrong—or are they?
- I wish they'd like me, but if they don't I'll manage—I'm in authority.

MY OBJECTIVES
- Office running efficiently.

- Smoothly operating staff.
- Getting workload done.
- Advancing my position.

FACT FINDING

- Mistakes have been made. (Maybe a new system for checking is needed.)
- It's hard to identify exactly who is at fault.
- My boss gets infuriated by mistakes and comes down heavily on me.
- He'll lose confidence in me if I make an error. (An assumption.)
- He expects perfection. (Another assumption.)

ISSUES

- Worker dissatisfaction.
- Methods to use when a mistake is made.

NEEDS

- Mine—safety and security, esteem.
- Theirs—Am I paying sufficient attention to supplying their needs? When did I last pay a compliment? When did I allay someone's fear of being fired?

CLIMATE

- Have I been putting forth positive vibes?
- Can they count on my being supportive?
- If they seem remote and self-protective, have I responded with friendliness?
- Have I taken any responsibility for creating the climate?
- Am I afraid to seem weak if I try to create a positive climate?

PHILOSOPHY

- Could I be accused of a philosophy such as do unto others and beat it?
- In my negotiations with them, do they win as much as I do? Or am I creating situations where covering my tracks works to their disadvantage?
- What is the philosophy of my superior?

Such a self-negotiation would lead to a problem-solving orientation, a realization of the many levels of the problem for which she must assume at least part of the responsibility for solution.

In the case just stated, suspicion of her workers toward her may be a long time dying. A new way of performing, one that takes into account their needs, not just her own safety, has to be repetitive to be believable. In time, however, trust can be built, and joint sessions on error reduction could be instituted to the benefit of all.

If the big boss could be induced to stop the scare tactics that initiated the whole dance, the atmosphere would probably improve and turnover lessen.

Suspicion in the initial stages of a negotiation is not unreasonable. People do need to get to know each other in order to develop trust. But if suspicion becomes the overriding passion and steps are not taken to ameliorate it, human potential is wasted— in business, in the social milieu, in life!

Manipulation

Manipulation has a negative connotation. We don't like to be a victim of it and we like to think of ourselves as too ethical to use the technique on others. Yet realistically we may on occasion use it or allow it to be used.

How does understanding manipulation help us as negotiators? First of all, knowledge that someone is attempting to steer us in a particular direction gives us options. It may be advantageous to grant a wish or change our view. If we make this determination consciously, to advance the negotiation, we've lost nothing by being manipulated in the transaction. On the other hand, when we recognize an attempt to manipulate us, we can also resist more effectively. Invited for a country weekend of family togetherness, my friend found that her daughter was trying to manipulate her into sitting with the kids Saturday night while she and her husband popped into a neighborhood party for "a little while." Not wishing to play along with the suggestion, "I thought it would be fun for you and the kids to have some time alone together," my friend had the courage to express her desire to go to the party, too. Another sitter was procured and they all had a lovely evening.

We must recognize that our own attempts to manipulate, while they may gain a concession, or catch someone off guard, can also have damaging results. For one thing, the other side will eventually realize what has happened and try to get even. They may even terminate the relationship if trust and goodwill falter. But an even greater danger exists. Manipulation can become a habit, a way of handling people, a modus operandi. Sometimes it's even quite successful, if you subscribe to the philosophy that the end justifies the means.

Manipulators are not necessarily trying to hurt the negotiation or the participants. They are, however, primarily concerned only with their own needs. The skillful manipulator may get people to do the things he wishes but he doesn't build a relationship based on goodwill and eventual trust. People feel uneasy and resentful, and the next time they will be wary. Even if no effort to manipulate is contemplated they will assume, nonetheless, that one is coming.

Manipulation is a word that has been associated with women. This is understandable. In a subservient position this tactic is often the only means of dealing with power. If you flatter, lie, pretend admiration, remain silent when words cry to be spoken, dance to the tune of the other, you may gain favor. But this is a reacting mode and it doesn't do much for your self-esteem. (It doesn't add to your credibility either.)

Recognize those instances when you are being manipulative and try to be forthright instead. Remember, if your philosophy demands that everyone in a negotiation should win, then instead of manipulating you will focus on the satisfaction of needs. Results from such an effort will be long lasting and lay the groundwork for future negotiations.

Poor Self-Image

"Even in periods when I felt discrimination, I never felt second class. There was something wrong with the discriminators, not something wrong with me. I think this kind of belief keeps people going when they're having a hard time of it." *

—ROSALYN YALOW

If ever there was an area in which negotiation with yourself is your salvation it is in cultivating self-esteem. Self-esteem makes life a bed of roses instead of a brier patch. It's nothing you can buy, inherit or earn. Neither good looks, accomplishments, money nor talent can assure it. The fact that you are loved and respected

* Gilbert, Lynn, and Gaylen Moore. *Particular Passions: Talks with Women Who Have Shaped Our Lives* (New York: Clarkson N. Potter, Inc., 1982).

by many doesn't automatically produce self-confidence. To assume that somebody else can make you happy is to give away power. As women, we are taught to please others, but security is not built solely upon love and approval. "Security" is an illusion. The closest we can come to it is the knowledge that we can handle our lives without outside help.

Columnist Phyllis Rose recently told of the nightmares she had as a teacher trying to establish classroom discipline. Compounding her fear of failure was a false assumption: "I used to think that problems of self-esteem were peculiarly female," she wrote.* If women believe they are more prone to anxiety than men, it is because they often undervalue their potential and think less of their abilities. In actuality everyone suffers the discomfort of worry. If one accepts that fact, it's not so frightening when it occurs.

I, too, remember such dreams. Her article made me realize how widespread anxieties are. It's not just me, it's not just her, it's everyone. My latest dream went like this: I was about to do a seminar in San Francisco. The hotel setting was familiar. I've been in similar ones all over the United States, but in this dream I was pressed for time. Somehow I had overslept, the time for the presentation had arrived, and I was blindly rushing to the seminar room but could not find it. And the worst of it was, I was naked! Now, that's one that wakes you in a cold sweat.

The people who exhibit confidence are comfortable with themselves and their feelings. Therein lies their power. They don't need to blame others for the vicissitudes of life; more important, neither do they blame themselves. They have found the ultimate friend—oneself.

It doesn't solve every problem, but many hurdles are bypassed if you don't constantly have to make friends with yourself.

If, however, you don't feel self-assured, don't despair. The most important thing to remember is that everything changes—for the better, for the worse and back again. A small victory makes a difference in the way we perceive ourselves. Doing something new fortifies us further. Just living life adds wisdom and experience. Self-confidence grows from small events, and it doesn't matter from what point we start.

*"Hers," *New York Times*, March 22, 1984.

Stop Denigrating Yourself

Some reminders are helpful in reducing a pattern of self-denigration.

• Confront the list of shoulds and oughts hanging over your head. Don't berate yourself if you didn't write that thank-you note. Do it, even if it's late, and get it off your back—that's far more productive than getting mired in guilt.

• Stop belittling yourself. Don't compare yourself to other people, nor your accomplishments to theirs. Are you trying to prove your inadequacies to yourself? What for? Fight back at the first self-critical note. Dr. David Burns pinpoints the distortions in self-critical thinking.

Overgeneralization! I never do anything right.

All or nothing thinking! The memo wasn't perfect, so it was rotten.

Fortune-teller error! I know if I try to get the mortgage, I'll fail.

Mental filter! Dwelling on negative detail: But that one critic really panned the show.

Disqualifying the positive! "Oh, saving the dog's life was nothing."

Jumping to conclusions! He would reject me if I offered an alternative suggestion.

Mind reading! I can just tell she didn't like my suggestions.

Burns suggests that you write down self-critical thoughts as they occur. You will be amazed at their frequency. Realizing it should help to diminish negative thoughts—and improve your self-image in the process.*

Feeding into low self-esteem are the stereotypical ways in which a woman considers herself inferior to men:

• She accepts an interruption from a man.

• She listens more respectfully to men than to women.

• She seeks and respects the advice of men on technical matters, on things mechanical, and to confirm the validity of her decisions.

• She often does all the above despite protestations to the contrary.

* Dr. David Burns, *Feeling Good: The New Mood Therapy* (New York: William Morrow, 1980).

While centuries of playing a subordinate role confirmed these stereotypes in women's consciousness, the last twenty years have turned this image topsy-turvy. Women must take responsibility if they allow the stereotypes to perpetuate.

How to Build Self-Esteem

As we learn new skills, our own perspectives change. I can change a tire because I've learned to do it. It was more a mental hurdle than a mechanical problem. Because I was (and still am) all thumbs, it's slow and labored; I've had to do it several times to get this far. But I know it's something I no longer need help with. It's a good way to feel and a boost to my self-esteem.

People with a low self-image are unusually vulnerable to criticism. They automatically assume that the critic has authority. Questioning the source of your assumptions is the first step in building confidence. If you risk behaving in a new way, choosing your behavior rather than passively reacting, feelings can change too. Contrary to assuming that you've got to master confidence before you can take charge of situations, the opposite approach gets results as well. Action produces changes in attitudes.

There is no magic formula. You build self-esteem slowly and on a solid foundation of learning, achievement and the feedback from relationships.

As you start to orchestrate your own actions, you may be surprised to find out that others are not cheering you on. As a matter of fact you may observe that those who have dominated you will try to reverse your new trend in an effort to keep you in control. In other words, you're making an impact and someone is threatened by the new definition of a relationship. If you are really on your way to fuller independence of thought and action, make it easy for them, help them to save face, pay particular attention to creating a good climate—but don't slide back into the old ways. Your next attempt to implement independent action will be more difficult if someone is making an extra effort to forestall the change.

When you're feeling diminished, it seems preposterous to look ahead to a time when your self-esteem will be rising. But remember that it comes in increments and a little goes a long way to keep you climbing. When you inevitably have those moments of faulty judgment, lack of nerve, even failure, *don't punish yourself*. Try again. And again. In this quest for emancipating your spirit several things need to be kept in mind.

- Avoid critical people or call them to task when they get going on you.
- Don't apologize for yourself, not even to yourself.
- Risk speaking directly and saying what you mean. Sensitivity to climate and needs shouldn't prevent you from communicating directly. You won't kill a negotiation. As a matter of fact, your credibility will increase because people will be able to rely on your spoken word as a genuine expression of your thinking.
- Give compliments. You may be playing it so close to the vest that you're not aware of the hunger of others for validation. It may be hard for you to get the words out but grateful feedback will dispel hesitation next time.
- Take compliments gracefully.

When you get to be a skilled negotiator you'll find it no problem to admit lack of confidence in a particular situation. You'll simply ask for more time to make yourself an expert.

The Apology

If we are concerned with the climate of a negotiation, there will be times when an apology is in order. Many people wince at the thought, and some prefer to let the climate deteriorate rather than apologize. Why it should be such a difficult thing to do requires some analysis.

Macho Thinking

Some people feel that to apologize weakens them, shows a chink in their armor. What nonsense! Who among us can lay claim to such perfection? Surely, in our hearts, we know that to admit a failing doesn't diminish us irreparably. Yet for a reluctant apologizer there is a whole constellation of threats.

- They'll respect me less.
- They won't feel secure in relying on me in the future.
- They won't trust my future judgment.
- They'll reject me altogether.
- No longer will they hold me in esteem.
- They'll be furious and embarrass me on the spot.

- I don't want to admit to myself that I've done something warranting an apology.
- I'll get away with it without an apology and no one will be the wiser.

In other words, the person who cannot bear to extend an apology even when the gesture is clearly called for believes it would damage his image.

If women fear contempt when admitting a mistake, for men it is an even greater stumbling block. If they don't accept an apology, the other party gets an edge, and this is particularly threatening to a macho image.

Women more readily recognize the value to be had by restoring a positive climate and are willing to do so. Putting things to rights in the form of an apology is less punishing than contributing to a degenerating atmosphere.

Excuse Me for Living

However, women may be heir to the problems arising from another type of apology—the apology of abasement.

Some people seem to apologize just for being alive, for being in a certain spot, as a preface to offering an opinion, as the afterword of having contributed to a conversation. Such an apology is unjustified and gratuitous. It is the hallmark of people who are so hesitant in offering their views that they must apologize for their content. This is perceived as weakness, and rightfully so. It is as much an automatic way of reacting as is the macho style of the person who won't make any apology at all.

When to Apologize

How much more rewarding to negotiate with someone to whom an apology is instinctive when the situation genuinely calls for one.

Have they been inconsiderate, caused an inconvenience, failed to meet a commitment, been abusive? Infractions can range from irritating but inconsequential lapses such as being late for an appointment to important errors such as supplying erroneous figures in a report. In the case of the latter, an apology is not sufficient. Remedial action is implicit and should accompany the apology.

Here are some reminders that will be helpful to the person

making an apology, then some considerations for those who are the recipients of apologies.

How to Apologize

- Don't use a cliché when apologizing. Be conscious of each episode as a separate entity requiring a unique response. If you've made people uncomfortable or inconvenienced them, consider using an apology to restore a positive climate. Correctly done, it can put the negotiation back on the track.
- Don't apologize to gain sympathy. Make the statement and get on with the business at hand.
- Realize that an apology can be used against you. This realization should not deter you from the task but should put you on the alert to keep it brief and to the point, so as not to fortify your potential enemies. Besides, if you can build goodwill, the benefits will likely exceed any harm that might ensue as a result of your disclosure.
- Be prepared for embarrassment! Who relishes laying herself open to criticism? But if it is forthcoming, so what? At least feelings are on the table, not seething beneath the surface ready to emerge at the first sign of vulnerability on your part. Apology has the effect of disarming someone who might otherwise be thinking, "I'll get back at you, you S.O.B.!" Anyway, embarrassment might not be forthcoming. Instead, you may hear sighs of relief that the tension has been eased and the negotiation can resume its forward momentum.
- The repentant sinner is usually forgiven. What doesn't work is the apology that doesn't sound sincere, that starts off with "I was guilty, *but...*" Here, "but" is a verbal eraser.

Apologize directly and personally rather than putting it on the record. Clear the decks once and for all and get back to the serious work of negotiating. To apologize is to seem vulnerable. You have to be strong to admit mistakes and even stronger to deal with the consequences. But it can be more punishing not to apologize than to admit a mistake.

How to Receive an Apology

If you are the recipient of an apology you have certain obligations to meet.

- It's helpful for the person who has risked extending the apology if you acknowledge it with a few words of appreciation prior to the resumption of negotiation. He will be grateful for your reciprocal offering that allows him to save face.

- Recognize that your acceptance of the apology will fulfill your opponent's need for reassurance that your relationship will continue.
- Recognize that men have problems in extending apologies and that even if they do, the offering is liable to be cursory. You can be generous when you receive an apology that is oblique. The offering may be less than sufficient to salve your wounded pride, but it may be a self-conscious attempt to right things and all that party is capable of at the moment. Very often the apology is no more than a humorous attempt to soothe the wound, but it is an acknowledgment of sorts. Accept it graciously.

Sometimes an entire negotiation hinges on your response to an apology. If you are feeling such strong anger or hurt that you are inclined to reject it, take the time to do a *thorough* mental review of your objectives. That in itself will likely give the validation needed to accept the apology and resume the negotiation. A positive climate can be restored, if you allow it.

Perfectionism, Procrastination and Avoiding Decisions

Getting ahead in this competitive world often demands hard work, long hours and pushing oneself to perform tasks of ever-increasing complexity. It is not easy. Among the problems that inhibit our ability to work and grow, three of the more troublesome are perfectionism, procrastination and difficulty in making decisions.

The newcomer to any field is most prone to these hazards. Lack of experience, not knowing the ropes, and ignorance of "the rules" all inhibit decision-making and promote perfectionism and procrastination; therefore women often fall prey to them in the rough and tumble of the business world. If you allow them to dominate your negotiating behavior, you will never learn to act effectively.

Perhaps this is a good time to play "what if": What if the speech I make at that meeting doesn't convince everybody? It's my job to fire the accountant but I've been putting it off—what if I just get it over with? What if I decide to stand up to that bully who's been taking verbal jabs at me?

In each instance, the result will not be earthshaking. If we expand our boundaries, try new skills, put ourselves on the line, it's risky and it may be painful, but we *grow*!

The Perfectionist

A perfectionist may not have problems with procrastination or making decisions but nonetheless may have a mind closed to alternatives and a manner that demands compliance. In negotiating, a perfectionist attitude prevents one from seeing the needs of other people and the necessity of addressing them, and therefore makes it that much more difficult to reach a negotiated outcome of any kind, much less one that satisfies both parties. There is a self-righteousness in perfectionism that may be productive for creating an artistic masterpiece, but is utterly inappropriate in the negotiating process. An artist has absolute control over all elements; such control is neither possible nor desirable in a negotiation.

The Procrastinator

A procrastinator may be capable of making decisions easily enough, and may not suffer from crippling perfectionism, yet may put off the necessary preparation for the negotiation until it's too late. So you go into it in a state of panic, with an off-the-top-of-my-head stance. You cannot depend on quick wit or luck to come to your rescue every time! The well-conceived alternative solutions you devise in advance are often the very elements that contribute to good agreements. To allow yourself to put off preparation beyond the point where you can do a really thorough job is to rob yourself of negotiating power. If you have been a procrastinator, use the negotiation map in its entirety, allowing yourself the time needed for this vital task. Your reward will be a new attitude toward your next negotiation and a self-confidence that will be recognized instantly by the other side.

Decisions, Decisions

You can't negotiate to a successful conclusion without making decisions about how to conduct the proceedings and when the time is ripe for closing. You will bog down if the risk of making a wrong decision panics you. Some decisions will indeed be wrong. However, the total negotiation rarely hinges on one unfortunate decision. Preparing thoroughly allows you to consider many alternatives, any one of which can be brought into play to retrieve a situation that is deteriorating. Being able to make decisions is imperative. Making wise decisions is a skill that tends to grow with experience.

In one of my college history classes, much anxiety among the students was centered on the writing of a lengthy essay that would significantly determine the grade point average for each of us. I wish I could remember the name of the wise professor who offered us a sensible adage, one I recall often when I need to galvanize myself to action. I'd like to thank him. He said, "The best is the enemy of the good," and this gave me comfort and the courage to proceed. I didn't need to be best. I wanted to do a good job. But most of all, I needed to *do* it!

This one line is, for me, a reminder that perfectionism procrastination and fear of making a decision can be dealt with. Gaining perspective helps me to know that important results do not hinge on every little thing I do.

Excuses

Everyone makes excuses at times to protect the feelings of others or, more likely, to rationalize a particular action of their own. Indeed, difficult moments that might otherwise bring about an open breech can be sidestepped with the help of a few soothing words offered up at the proper time.

• Darned if I didn't get a flat right on the highway. Couldn't even call you. Sorry for the delay.

• My office forgot to give me your message. Otherwise I would have gotten back to you sooner with the figures.

• My back is acting up. I'll never last the five hours of *Götterdämmerung*. I love Wagner but I'll have to slip out at intermission.

If the explanation is accepted, the negotiation proceeds despite the annoyance.

Someone who doesn't have enough social finesse to make any excuses is a boor who tramples on people's feelings, sometimes without even recognizing the effects that his lack of tact is having. One particularly inept socializer, when saying goodnight to his date, said, "I won't call you again because I'm going to try going out with a good-looking girl for a change!" (This actually happened!) Obviously, there's something terribly lacking in the person who is so out of tune with people's sensibilities.

There's always the danger that an excuse will backfire. Sometimes a third party will step in to soothe someone's hurt. One day my youngest son came running into the house, obviously furious. "I hate Ritchie," he fumed. "He stinks!" I felt obligated to say something only because I was sitting with Ritchie's mother at the time. This was one time when I should have left well enough alone. Instead, to mollify my friend and excuse my son, I said, "Oh, you don't really mean that, George. You know you like Ritchie. You just had a fight." In a perfect fury he nullified my soothing attempt. "Yes, I do mean it. I hate him, and so do you! You told me he was a brat!" So much for intervention.

Have You Counted Them Lately?

Whether excuses are being made in a business or personal setting, it's wise to monitor yourself and get an accurate reading of how often and under what circumstances you resort to making them. Are the excuses becoming more daring and outlandish? Can you judge the effect on others? Are others buying your excuses or is a note of skepticism creeping in? Resort to pen and paper to track your excuse quotient. There are problems to be dealt with if the incidence is on the rise. A week's notation can give insight into the way you've been handling your negotiations. Likely you are making excuses in self-defense to avoid criticism. If this is so ask yourself why someone's disapproval is so threatening that you can't hit it head on, take it in stride if the complaint is genuine, and move on to the next order of business.

- Was I late with the report because I'm lazy?
- Did I arrive too late for the tryouts because I was afraid to risk my self-esteem?
- Did I refuse to back up John's figures because I'm more secure being noncommittal?
- Did I put the onus on my husband, accusing him of extreme provocation, to excuse my own lapse of behavior?
- Did I make excuses for what I feel was an inadequate dinner,

warding off anticipated criticism even though it wasn't forth-coming?

Making excuses to others is a protective device and its use-fulness is limited by how often people are willing to accept them. In the business setting, if the frequency increases, you'll get pegged as an unreliable negotiator. If you must use them, be sure to back them up with hard data lest your credibility suffer. A reliance on excuses exhibits a weakness that erodes the confidence people have in you and hampers future negotiations with them.

More damaging is the phenomenon of making excuses to yourself, of rationalizing an act you're not proud of by excusing yourself. To rationalize each time such an event transpires may give you the false luxury of putting an end to the episode; it also prevents you from the self-examination that is the first step to change.

The self-confident person doesn't feel the need to make ex-cuses. If she is wrong, she admits it. If she isn't dressed to the hilt, she doesn't excuse herself when she appears in public. She just is! She pays herself the greatest compliment in being herself, whoever that is, and accepting that person. This is the frame of mind that allows change to take place, unencumbered by the constant need to be self-protective.

We all make excuses, but making them too often is counter-productive. It doesn't bolster our image, it destroys it. Pay at-tention to frequency and reduce the incidence if you need to.

Criticism

"People ask you for criticism, but they only want praise."
—SOMERSET MAUGHAM

It's hard to know which is more painful: having to dish out criticism or being the recipient of it. One thing is sure, neither is a pleasure.

Everyone resents being criticized, women no more than men. What particularly rankles, however, is criticism based more on a preconceived stereotype than on the actual situation. You're too emotional. You change your mind all the time. You're acting just like a woman. These pronouncements could apply to men as well but unfairly enough are usually reserved for women.

Apart from having to cope with such unproductive put-downs it's often difficult for women to mete out criticism. And it's often difficult for men to accept it from women. They may even perceive a differing viewpoint as critical, making women particularly cautious not to offend.

Whichever end you're at—giving or receiving—if you consider criticism as a negotiating situation as well as a negotiating tool, it becomes more manageable. This is an instance when it is particularly important to think things through from the viewpoint of the opposite side; then conduct the negotiation as expeditiously as possible and get on with life, egos intact.

Let's look at criticism first from the point of view of one who is giving it and then from the opposite perspective, that of the recipient.

Giving Criticism

Some critics seem not to be troubled about chewing someone out. They appear to go for the jugular in order to make their points. More than likely they're in a position of presumed power. I'm hard put to recall an instance in which I've seen a worker openly criticize a boss and hope to remain on the job. Who can afford such a luxury?

In personal relationships, harmony in daily living is at stake. Yet individuals are often hurtful in their criticism without thinking of the effect their words will have. Whether in a personal or a business context, criticism often comes off as a personal attack. Think what your own gut reactions might be to the following:

"If you had moved the car when I told you to, it wouldn't have been towed away. Your problem is you don't listen! And you don't listen because you don't care!"

"You're inefficient! When are you going to get this place organized? It looks like a pigsty!"

"You're insulting just like your father! I don't have to take this nonsense!"

"If you knew how to give orders, the copying would have been done by 4 P.M. But you don't know how to handle people!"

"You lost the account because of your goddamned procrastination! You should have gotten the bid in, but you let it bog down at the planning stage—just like you did last year when we lost the crack at the hotel campaign."

These criticisms, however indelicate, may indeed be valid and necessary. At issue is the manner in which they are delivered; and therein lies the negotiation.

You, as the person doing the criticizing, should ask yourself some fundamental questions. First, have you negotiated with yourself to understand what you're feeling and the implications for all parties when your emotions dictate action? No? Then do it now!! Take a hard look before you give in to that impulse to clobber. Your investigation into your own thinking might be stimulated by questions such as the ones that follow. Many more will occur to you if you have the courage to be firm in the quest! Before you criticize, open yourself to some self-criticism because, when you think of it, *you* are the only person you'll accept criticism from anyway.

- What am I getting from being critical? Power? (The power I feel in seeing someone cringe?)
- What do I really want? Resolution or more conflict? (Sometimes ongoing bitterness is psychologically preferable to dealing with the problem. You may be fearful that the solution will possibly end the active relationship.)
- What's my righteousness quotient? (Am I getting pleasure from being "right," from seeing the situation only from the perspective of facts I can line up to substantiate my view?)
- Do I feel superior to the other person when I criticize? (If I point out deficiencies, does that not imply that I could do better, and thus am superior?)
- Do I criticize to excess? Has it become habitual? (Is my action automatic rather than the result of thought? Is this way of acting becoming part of my personality?)
- Do I repeat a critical stance despite adverse reaction to it?
- Do I criticize to ward off criticism of me? ("The best defense is a good offense" syndrome.)
- Is my motive to control or intimidate?
- Am I open or sneaky in my approach?
- If, indeed, I have been using criticism as a strategy in a negotiation, have I lost sight of the climate? Is it deteriorating?

After subjecting yourself to such an inquisition you may be forced, at the very least, to accept some responsibility for the give-and-take of a situation in which criticism is being shelled out by you. One significant question must be recalled. *What are my objectives?* If the way in which you are offering the criticism (whether deserved or not) has an adverse effect on gaining your objectives, stop. Find another way of operating; your use of the negotiating map will point the way to alternative behaviors.

Do

- *Avoid personal assaults.* Deal with the action, not the person. "You're inefficient," "you don't know how to handle people," "your goddamn procrastination," and "just like your father" are destructive statements.
- *Preface criticism with some explanation of its purpose.* That makes what follows understandable and gives the recipient time to muster survival techniques.
- *Criticize in private.* If you cause employees to lose face, they will have no incentive to put forth their best effort.
- *Be specific on points of criticism* so that the other party understands clearly what you mean. "Your work is not up to par" is not helpful. "The last two reports were late and I expect you to meet deadlines" gives more information.
- *Agree on methods to deal with the problem.* Gain the commitment of the other party.
- *Be honest about the consequences if change doesn't occur.*
- *End on a positive note.* This will make it easier for the person being criticized not to be defensive.
- *Give the person time to correct the error* but limit the time frame so the parameters are specific.
- *Set up another meeting* to make sure the matter is now being handled satisfactorily.
- *Be available to assist* with any problems that occur during the correction period.

Don't

- Attack the person.
- Criticize in front of other people.
- Insult.
- Degrade.
- Yell.
- Let the climate deteriorate.
- Use innuendo. Don't pussyfoot to soften the blow. Have the courage to be direct.

- Make the other feel guilty. It will surely backfire.
- Make someone feel small to make yourself big.
- Focus on blame but on ways to make the situation better.

What if I can train myself not to give criticism? Won't I and those with whom I come in contact be better off? Not necessarily. If you are acting in a supervisory capacity, you will sometimes have to step on other people's toes. You don't have a choice! In personal matters, criticism is more delicate and must be treated with caution. Presuming there is a legitimate rationale rather than the desire to wound, what's so terrible about putting grievances on the table? As in so many cases, it's a matter of the method, the timing, the will to make it better for everyone, not just yourself.

You don't die from having to be critical. And you don't die from being criticized. As a matter of fact, many women in business feel disadvantaged by not receiving the same criticism a man would in a similar position. They feel it retards their progress and would prefer to be on an equal footing, even in so dubious a pleasure as . . .

Taking Flak

If the criticism is legitimate, take it. Don't try to diffuse the blame. A boss will recognize and appreciate the attitude of one who accepts the need to make corrections and puts energy into that task. If, on the other hand, the criticism is unwarranted, your defense of yourself should not begin with a statement that she's wrong! Deference to her position as boss necessitates more tact from you than she was gracious enough to display. Acknowledge that you realize she's upset, acknowledge that she thinks you're at the basis of this problem, and only then plead your case. Her position will not allow her to tolerate a direct challenge but she will cool down quicker if you follow an approach that protects the climate. You are not a doormat that must take abuse! State your case, of course. But do it in such a way that your objectives are well served.

Some people criticize others in so harsh a fashion that they elicit not only fear but a great deal of anger as well. If you've been in such a work situation you can assess whether this abuse is a personal assault or whether it's just a way of reacting to a frustrating situation. It's darned irritating in either case, but produces less tension if you can rationalize that this is your day for getting it and tomorrow somebody else will have the pleasure. It's not likely that the abuser's behavior will change, but properly dealt with it can improve. Whether you wish to adjust is a choice you must make. It's a matter of degree; there is a point beyond which another job might be a better bet.

Criticism, in the final analysis, while sometimes necessary, is difficult to administer and difficult to take. Whichever end of it you're on, if you treat it as a negotiation, you will make it more manageable. Counting to ten, that well-worn cliché, will help you hold back the barrage. During this breather, think "Map." Quickly review your objectives, the needs on either side, the facts as you know them, the climate in the making. This quick review may point the way to an altered approach, one in which the dignity of all parties can be maintained while yet getting your point across.

In personal relationships, habitual criticism is extremely counterproductive. Constant carping, picking at wounds, nagging, benefits nobody. But habits die hard. When emotions are high, you're at greater risk and more likely to use criticism as an attack, losing sight of your aims. Your self-negotiation will tell you whether you're falling prey to such destructive patterns.

"Criticism," said Ralph Waldo Emerson, "should not be querulous and wasting, all knife and root-puller, but guiding, instructive, inspiring—a south wind, not an east wind."

The Hidden Assumptions in Our Sex Roles

Most of us have sex-role-stereotyped beliefs which we carry with us from childhood. This is true for both men and women and many of these hidden assumptions are vestiges from a more traditional era. Although many women may consider themselves "liberated" because they are professionals or go to business, some recognize that they are hampered in personal relations and business negotiations by the sex-role assumptions which they themselves hold and which are held by men.

These hidden assumptions can create feelings of dissatisfaction, harassment and discrimination, all of which lead to barriers in the negotiating process.

Some Common Female Assumptions

The woman who is entering or returning to the work arena must do some negotiating with herself to discover what her own assumptions are about her role and needs.

If she assumes that her role as housewife and mother cannot be sacrificed to her work outside the home or if she feels a compulsion to do both equally well, she may find herself in a state of constant fatigue and irritability. However, if she discovers that her compulsion to keep an immaculate house results from her *assumption* that it is her appropriate role, a further inquiry might reveal that her mate is perfectly willing to share such tasks.

A woman professor of my acquaintance held such an antipathy for the traditional role that she would not marry until she got a commitment from a man to take over all the household tasks. She was successful in negotiating just such an arrangement with her husband, who happily took over all the cooking, shopping and household tasks and shared the child-rearing responsibilities, to the satisfaction of both of them.

On the other hand, there are still some women who believe that the only way they will achieve the things they want in life is under the aegis of a man.

The other day, I shared a taxi with a chatty young woman. As we drove through the prosperous section of our town, she pointed to several of the mansions we were passing and said, "One of these days, I'm going to live in one of those houses—when I marry a rich man!" I marveled not only at her certainty that she would, but at her assumption that that was the only way she would achieve it. I also feared for this young woman, who may one day find herself at the not-so-tender mercies of a husband who no longer wants to support her fantasy of being pampered and cared for, but wants someone who is self-reliant and competent.

If a woman's role image causes her to fear success or to regard her work outside the home as a job and not a career, she puts limits on the exploration of opportunities which may be presented. She must seriously review her objectives before presenting herself to a prospective employer lest she reveal her ambivalence or he may not take her seriously as a member of the team with potential for advancement.

The liberated woman, unfettered by assumptions about her sex role, who makes choices for herself despite current fads, fashions or mores, whether such choice is to be at home to raise children or to seek a career, can better deal with the challenge of men's hidden assumptions.

Some Assumptions Held by Men

Some men, too, hold sex role stereotypes which hark back to another era. They cling to the old ideas: A woman's place is in the home; it is unfeminine for a woman to compete with a man; a woman is not competent to compete with men in scientific, mechanical and mathematical matters. They see themselves as the family providers and authority figures. Their masculinity is threatened when their wives go out to work or if they are asked by their wives to share in household chores or the care of the children. They expect that, as the primary breadwinners, where they go the wife must follow, even if she must give up a satisfying career.

With more wives going back to school or into the job market or the professions, negotiations between husbands and wives must be reviewed with attention to the esteem needs of the husband. If a woman marries a man whose assumption is that a woman's place is in the home, it does no good to call him a troglodyte because she has changed and he has not. He might be persuaded to a change of view if a higher-order need such as the economic gain to both through the wife's contribution of income is stressed. He may also achieve a healthier regard for his wife's efforts if and when he recognizes that his assumptions about her role as a woman are not inviolate.

In the workplace men are also being forced to examine their assumptions about a woman's role. The subordinate, subservient role of women is changing rapidly. The cry of sex discrimination has made men think twice about once acceptable practices. Unless they or other males in the firm have exhibited a willingness to share in making coffee, they hesitate to ask a woman to do it unless this is one of her duties that was clearly spelled out when she was hired.

As women seek equal partnership, equal pay and equal opportunity, men who continue to see women as sex objects or mother substitutes in the workplace will feel that something has been taken away from them and express resentment. These men often turn a deaf ear to women who are their peers at board meetings and conferences. They do not pay attention to the suggestions, proposals or advice given by women, and only when these same have been reiterated by a man (who now takes full credit for the utterance) a few minutes later, do they accept what is being said. If this situation happens repeatedly, a woman must ask herself whether it is her manner of presentation which causes it, or whether it is indeed an aspect of sex discrimination. She may have to resort to finding a male ally who will repeat her suggestions while giving her credit for them. She may find the sex role attitude at the upper echelons of management so engrained that her competence is not recognized or rewarded. She must then decide whether to present her case before a sex discrimination agency or to consider that her situation represents a dead end and that it is time to move on.

If, at a negotiation, a woman recognizes that the man opposite her is exhibiting a dismissive attitude, her best strategies are complete preparation and unemotional attention to the business at hand. The best acknowledgment she will get from such an opponent is that she conducts herself "just like a man."

Each of us must examine those assumptions—I am helpless to change my situation, I am a failure, that's a man's job, a woman's place, etc.—which distort our lives and cause us needless distress.

When we hear ourselves say, "I can't," we must ask ourselves why not and ferret out those beliefs and assumptions which stifle our creative thinking or strangle our efforts to do the possible. One of those assumptions we can readily dispel is that we can't because we are women.

Failing to Listen

"One of the best ways to persuade others is with your ears—by listening to them."

—DEAN RUSK

We listen, but are we getting the message? We talk, but is anyone listening to us? When we fail to pay attention the negotiation process suffers. On the other hand, "Why isn't he listening to me?" or "What I say to him goes in one ear and out the other" are sad refrains, frequently heard.

It is probably not only conventional wisdom, but true, that women are better, more sympathetic listeners than men are. However, in a negotiating situation, a woman who is not a skilled negotiator may be so concerned about her own performance, or how to counter the last point that was made, that she may not be listening to what is being said *now*. She may not only be missing something important, but her lack of attention is probably affecting the climate—for the worse.

Developing Listening Skills

Listening skills can be developed. Here are some suggested means:

• Take time to listen. When you see a display of emotion recognize that person's need to talk things out.
• Be attentive. Concentrate on what is being said and use gestures such as tilting the head to indicate nonverbally that you are paying attention.
• Give feedback. Often a smile or a nod of the head is more effective than words and allows the other person to complete a thought.
• Don't be critical and don't pass judgment. This cuts off avenues of communication.
• Refrain from giving advice unless it is your professional advice that is sought.
• Respect the speaker and her worth. This will allow the speaker to feel that what she is saying is important and protect her self-esteem.

Effective listening is a means toward creating a supportive climate, that all-important component in a successful negotiation.

Getting Others, Particularly Men, to Listen

Women complain that men don't listen to them. On the job they feel that a man's opinion carries more weight than a woman's, the issues notwithstanding. On the home front, the complaint is, "He tunes me out." What rankles most is that he may not even be aware that he is doing it.

It is a real problem, rooted in many of the customs and stereotypes that men and women carry around with them.

• Some men genuinely feel that a woman's contribution is negligible, and so they do not indeed bother to listen.

- It may be a matter of style: Is your tone hesitant? Too deferring? Voice too low to be heard easily? Are your statements tentative? Are you easily silenced by a put-down?
- Men may be less interested in discussing topics that interest women, such as relationships.
- Some men are not interested in small talk. If you don't keep to the point, their attention wanders.

What can women do to change these habits?

Do

- Be succinct. Why should anyone pay attention to a long-winded story that doesn't have a useful message for the listener?
- Organize your thoughts so your delivery of the message is easy to grasp.
- Pay attention to voice tone, intonation and pitch. Sometimes raising or lowering your voice will capture an ear.
- Make eye contact with people you're addressing.
- Watch your gestures to indicate openness and enthusiasm for what you express.
- Speak appropriately. A business meeting is not the place for a family anecdote, no matter how amusing, unless it serves a definite purpose.
- Learn to ask questions effectively to focus attention on yourself.
- Satisfy your listener's need to know and understand.

Don't

- Use technical jargon. If you can't avoid it, explain your terms.
- Interject at inappropriate moments.
- Assault people personally or put them on the defensive.
- Neglect the environment. Subject a nonsmoker to a smoke-filled room and she is more tuned in to discomfort than to what is being said.
- Hog the floor. Know when to quit talking.

Prior Success

Our prior successes may be a barrier if we are afraid to change the formula and try something new. A woman who acts helpless may often get people to do things for her, but it's courting disaster if she has no alternatives prepared for those situations in which no one responds. Conversely, the mothering type, who prides herself on her ability to hold up the world and does indeed work very hard to keep things rolling, may find that her managerial efforts are sometimes resisted because they are seen as efforts to control. At this point, benign neglect might be more successful.

It is also risky to repeat other people's successful patterns without understanding them. For example, you decide to imitate a successful technique of your favorite negotiator—splitting the difference. The next time you represent someone, you suggest that the parties split the difference in the price. Instead of gratitude, you get outrage. "Why didn't you state the real price in the first place?" you are asked. With egg on your face you wonder why the technique didn't work for you. Perhaps in this case you were premature. You may not have allowed sufficient time to elapse; the parties may not have been sufficiently anxious before you made your proposal. A tried and true technique can boomerang if the timing is wrong. No two situations are the same.

If your negotiation has become familiar routine and you think you know just what's going to happen because you've done it so many times before, you are in danger of getting caught napping when some abrupt unexpected change occurs. Be prepared to see the differences in every situation rather than the similarities. Bring some lively, creative energy to every encounter to foster growth rather than entropy.

Don't depend on strategies and tactics just because they've worked once before. Instead, as you prepare for your presentation or negotiation, be open-minded to all potential negotiating strategies.

Bottom Line

"The tendency to boil the world down into analytic abstractions distorts and oversimplifies the richness of life. It insists upon evaluating the world through ratings and lists, matrices and pools, the bottom line, winners and losers."*

"You have no doubt encountered people who impatiently wait for the payoff. They urge you to come to the point at dinner, the

*Norman Lear, "Bottom Linesmanship," in *The New York Times*, May 20, 1984.

early courses merely delay dessert; they look only at the bottom line (that obscene phrase). They are persons consumed by consequences; they want to climax without crescendo."*

We've all run into the situation in which we meander through a conversation, trying to clarify our thinking, only to be cut off by an impatient person who says, "Yes, but what's the bottom line?" This is not only humiliating, but it usually has a stultifying effect on the exchange. When we force bottom-line thinking on ourselves, we tend to limit our options.

If you define $250,000 as the bottom-line price you want for your house, you may have closed your mind to terms that might make a lower price more beneficial. How about the new owner fixing that roof problem? Maybe you need leeway in moving time to establish a new residence. Maybe what you really need is "all cash." Even if you *use* the expression "bottom line," your mind should be open to the myriad possibilities that present themselves during the course of a negotiation. Everything is changing in this process world and any factor that closes your thinking or hinders exploratory communication may stunt the deal.

In a personal relationship, the bottom line concept is even more dangerous because the issues are not likely to be quantifiable like the price of a house. Attitudes, feelings and aspects of self-image are brought into play and need to be dealt with. Bottom line is too strong a stance to take on a personal issue. If the other person doesn't respond satisfactorily to your bottom line (which is probably in the nature of an ultimatum), what next? Your guess is as good as ours. Where was your consideration of the climate you were creating? What about needs, theirs and yours? Did you think about what tactics might be used to counter your strategy of deadline? Did you think these things through at all? Did you count to ten before you started?

In all negotiations, business or personal, boxing yourself into a position is highly risky. For instance, if you say, "Either we go skiing or forget vacation this year," you may be creating a situation in which nobody wins. Not only may everyone have to forgo a vacation, but the climate of the relationship will deteriorate, at least temporarily. Further consideration might make you reconsider not the value but the cost of bottom-line thinking.

*William Gass, in The New York Times, April 1, 1984.

The Limits of Advice

Very often, advice that people give puts you on the defensive. "Why don't you wear the blue bag? It would look much better than that thing." "If you take my advice you'll go right in there and complain to the boss." "Why do you take that? I wouldn't let a kid talk to me that way." Often this advice comes unsolicited and makes you feel inadequate in some way.

Why do some people relish giving advice? To bolster their own feelings of superiority? To put you down? To exercise control over you? To be helpful? Is it simply habit? The reasons are many, and most of them are hidden, especially from the person from whom the advice keeps coming. Are you perhaps one of these gratuitous advisers? What reactions do you get?

Is It Really Advice?

If a discussion of advice begins to sound like an analysis of criticism, it's because they are often interchangeable. No wonder advice is so often resented. I have a friend whose style it is to advise, to guide, to better, to help—and to nag. That's the way I perceive it. When she comes to visit, with her kindly suggestions in tow, I can't help anticipating the first jab. Perhaps it will be, "If I were you, I'd use another tablecloth. That color isn't right." After the table is set. Or, "Why did you decide on vertical blinds? This room really calls for a more formal look. Drapes would look better." After the blinds are installed, of course. She just doesn't know how to let things be. As a result, people bristle and tend to avoid her, even though the advice is often valid and might be useful.

I, as a friend, have been remiss in this situation by taking the path of least resistance, not bothering to tell her what I'm feeling so that the air can be cleared. It's not that big an issue and it could be successfully negotiated. She might be insulted or even momentarily angry, but if the proper tone is set both parties will know where they're at the next time.

When and How

I think my experience with such advice givers has sensitized me to the adverse reactions such offerings can engender and I am loath to offer advice, unless asked. But a dilemma results. There are occasions in which one is witness to a situation just begging for advice. To stand on neutral ground is to avoid responsibility.

Would you let a friend berate her husband in public without privately discussing the possible ramifications with her? Take the risk, say your piece. If you relate it to your own experience, telling the good things as well as the bad, it will seem less threatening. Don't make it a habit, expect to be resented, and don't beat a dead horse. If you harp on it too long you will risk a rupture in the relationship.

In responding to a request for advice the same ground rules apply. Ask yourself why this advice is sought before you plunge into giving it. Are hard data being sought? Are you being asked to advise on the choices for a course of action? Is it hoped that your advice will simply confirm a decision that has already been made, or are you not really being asked for advice at all? Often a person needs a sounding board, a listener to hear one out so ideas can crystallize sufficiently and paths of action become apparent. You, as listener with a sympathetic ear, showing interest and involvement, can be a catalyst in the process.

In a negotiation, whether it be an informal, interpersonal kind or an across-the-table business variety, there are certain useful things to remember when giving or taking advice.

AS A RECEIVER
- Try to figure out the motive and the need of the adviser.
- Acknowledge that need. If it is a need for esteem, find a way to show that you value that person. If his love and belonging needs are prompting the advice, show his importance to you.
- Don't react in a defensive manner, even if you perceive the advice as criticism.
- Deliberately maintain a positive climate. Try to understand critical advice instead of merely refuting it. Find out where the other person is coming from, intellectually as well as emotionally.

AS A GIVER OF ADVICE
- Ask yourself what your motive is: to control, to be helpful, to avert disaster?
- Try to intuit the response your advice will bring.
- Have you been asked to comment at all? Be clear on this before you offer your opinion.

Difficult People

You can't handpick the people you negotiate with. It's naive to hope for a friendly, helpful, accommodating opponent. Very often, you get just the opposite; a personality who is difficult to deal with.

It's just as naive not to recognize that you may be difficult yourself. Your opponent has to deal with your character quirks and may be hard pressed to find the way to interact with you.

It is important to keep in mind that the purpose of a negotiation is to change relationships, not individuals. Changing relationships may change people, but you can't count on it. You take what you get and you deal with it.

There are many varieties of difficult people. We will describe some in this chapter, and provide some tips about how to recognize and cope with them. However, in dealing with difficult personalities, it is always useful to keep the negotiation map in mind.

Are You Difficult?

If you begin properly by negotiating with yourself, you may discover that *you* are the one who is being difficult.

"What do you mean, what time is it? Are you suggesting that I'm goofing off?" In making such a statement, you are clearly being defensive, somewhat hostile and defiant to boot. Without finding out what your supervisor intended in asking the question, you reacted as if you had been challenged. Is this the way you usually react if you sense disapproval? Overreaction? Is it possible that you are a difficult person?

"I always get the worst assignments." Do you play martyr and victim in an effort to gain sympathy or instill guilt, or simply to get some loving attention? If this is your style others will consider you difficult.

"I don't care if you said you'd meet them at Fun Lee Palace. I'm not going. I don't like their food!" Is this a burst of temperament? Are you being arbitrarily petulant? Are you a spoiler? What are your hidden agendas? Are you a difficult person on this particular evening?

All of us indulge in occasional outbursts that are atypical. We can be forgiven such lapses. If, however, you find that you're locked into habit patterns, it's time to modify your behavior. Not easy. Try to recognize the critical moment. Then stop in your tracks before you act. Having broken the impulse to react in your habitual way you can consciously choose your response. Perhaps it will be the same. Perhaps not.

It is easier to pinpoint an unattractive behavior trait in others than in ourselves. So, a greater effort needs to be made to monitor our own actions.

When Others Are Difficult

When you start to assess another person's behavior, remember to use the technique of "dating." She is disagreeing with every statement I make—today. Next week the situation may change. You must not judge her a negative person, except for today.

Difficult people come in many guises and we don't necessarily recognize them at the onset of a negotiation. If you've ever had dealings with a con artist, you know that charm and plausibility are tools that this manipulator uses with exquisite perfection. He can keep you smiling even as he induces you to go against your own best interests. Resentment sets in later, but if he's really slick he may even fool you again. Typically, he does this by appealing to greed—that great deal you would be crazy to miss out on, but which you would find out is pie in the sky if only you took the time to investigate.

Another variety of amiable but difficult negotiator is one who can't say no, who ingratiates himself by his friendliness and interest, and agrees to your terms, never planning to deliver.

Since his interests seem to parallel your own and he has made you feel that there will be no hitches to a mutually successful outcome, it's easy to fall into the trap. You ease up on your preparation and neglect to unearth his previous track record, which would have revealed that, as an agent with limited authority, he doesn't even have the clout to close a deal.

It does no good to ask *why* someone is difficult. It *does* help to see the behavior in a context. Women are learning to separate their personal reactions to people from the body of the negotiation. Every argument doesn't have to be dissected and ironed out for a working arrangement to continue. Watch how other people react to unpleasant behavior. What ticks me off might not bother you at all. What someone else might consider a gross insult might roll off my back easily. Someone listening to my son making a request of me said, "Why do you let him speak to you that way?" "What way?" I asked. She had heard it as an imperious demand that should have been challenged. Maybe so, but I perceived it in a way that allowed me to fulfill his request without getting defensive about the exact manner in which it was made. It is helpful to acknowledge our own complicity—a precipitating action or oversight that brings about the very behavior we're complaining about.

It is not the behavior that's important but the manner in which we react to it. Easygoing people are not pushovers. They stand up for themselves with as much fervor as the bravest of us, but not all the time and not from a sense of insecurity. Because they accept many styles of behavior they can be more cooperative and are less likely to create issues over minor points, since they don't bring emotion to every detail. If your opponent is such a negotiator, you're in luck. A lot of ego maneuvers can be dispensed with.

Unfortunately, not many of us are that able to keep our cool. A personal attack is quite disorienting. Because of the embarrassment and humiliation you experience you feel called upon to respond in a way that will restore your self-respect and credibility. You haven't time, in such an instance, to figure out the intent of the offender. Is it political, is it a personal vendetta, is it an effort to weaken your position? When you're reeling from such a blow and all eyes are on you, judging your mettle, it is a dangerous moment in a negotiation. If you crumble and take abuse just to put an end to the unfortunate instant, you have said, in effect, that you will tolerate a tirade rather than negotiate it. Like Neville Chamberlain dealing with Adolf Hitler, you play the role of appeaser—with similar results.

Is your better choice to give it to him in spades, turn his own tactics back on him and scream louder?

This approach will polarize issues, fix positions into two armed camps and leave no room for face-saving at either end. If you are in a subordinate position, it's insubordination. If you are equals, it's escalated warfare.

Neither back down nor strike out. Stand your ground—literally! Don't lose eye contact. State your opinions whenever you can interject them, but refuse to argue the issue—now. Don't be bullied into making a decision on the spot and state your intention not to do so. Recognize that there is a personality problem quite aside from the objective merits of the negotiation itself.

Do what you can to defuse the situation. Take a break, substitute another spokesman, arrange a time when you can unravel emotional knots in private, forbear—wait it out.

When the moment of crisis passes and tempers subside, accommodations are possible. Goodwill, hesitant but respectful, can result.

Remember the Concept of Change

Try to focus not on the person but on the behavior itself, and deal with that. The same person who gives you a hard time this month may be easy to deal with next. If you can maintain communication, you might be able to arrive at a rapprochement. Crises in her life may have been resolved, allowing her to relinquish the hostile or defensive actions that had made the association a difficult one. If you label her difficult, you may not allow her the freedom to change her behavior toward you because your energy will go into proving yourself right, rather than into righting the relationship.

Sometimes it's hard to tell whether you are dealing with difficult people or difficult circumstances. Too often we assign the label "difficult" to the people we're negotiating with to avoid dealing with the specifics of the negotiation. It's important to keep the distinction clearly in mind.

The Spoiler

More than anyone else, the spoiler can frustrate you completely and make you wonder whether it's worth negotiating at all. He or she approaches any negotiation with a critical, sour, punishing attitude that is more concerned with finding fault than with achieving results. Think of all the elements of a good negotiation that are lost in such a transaction: satisfaction of needs, achievement of objectives, building of trust, goodwill, and possibilities for future exchanges.

Can you negotiate with someone of such a bent? The answer *must* be yes, simply because we don't always choose with whom we negotiate. You may not know beforehand that you've got a spoiler in your midst. Sometimes it's not even your opposite number, but someone on the fringe of the proceedings, who throws the monkey wrench.

How to Protect Yourself

However, if you know you are dealing with a spoiler, there are some ways to protect yourself:

- Secure all agreed-upon points in writing so as to document each of them.
- Arrange for witnesses to the proceedings to corroborate what has occurred and ensure that your reading of the territory is on target.
- Relinquish the luxury of spontaneity and carefully orchestrate your words, your questions, your pronouncements.
- Carefully refrain from using inflammatory statements or language. Stick to a descriptive mode of discourse.
- Do not broadcast your assessment of the person you're dealing with. She's already paranoid and any word of your ill will that reaches her ears will make the next session worse.
- Don't get trapped into a discussion of past grievances. It can only further exacerbate the situation.
- Never *react*; always *initiate* action. Your natural inclination to respond candidly and express your feelings is not productive in this instance. In terms of strategy, consider the value of forbearance. With such a person authentic communication is not the issue. You've got to keep yourself from drowning, and to this end you need to refrain from anything that might be inter-

preted as excess of any kind: talking, acting out, and so on.
- Maintain a positive climate as well as you can. Don't rise to
the bait when confronted with a cutting remark. The moment
your blood starts to boil, when you feel that nasty rejoinder on
your lips (the one that will really set her on her heels), *stop*, or
at least *wait*. You should be seeing the negotiation map in your
mind's eye. Think of your objectives, the anchor that will keep
you from damaging your cause for momentary emotional satisfaction.

Who's the Spoiler?

Have you negotiated with yourself to determine whether *you* are
the spoiler in this negotiation? The most difficult part of such an
examination is to acknowledge one's own contribution to the
conflict. We simply don't see in ourselves the fault we find glaring
in another. Zero in on your own emotional state. Jealous? Defiant?
Defensive? Are you talking behind people's backs? Do you make
cutting asides? Are you looking for someone to blame? Do you
feel righteous? If so, it's a true signal that you had better rethink
the whole negotiation and reconsider your role vis-à-vis needs
and climates because you're on the wrong track.

You yourself may be the spoiler.

The Pressure Cooker

What goes on in people who blow their tops? Are they being
purely aggressive? Do they like putting you down? Do they dislike
you? Are they trying to embarrass you?

Actually, someone who is set on such a course is not negotiating at all. She is displaying raw emotion, quite separate from
any thought-out plan for dealing with a situation. At that particular
moment *she is a difficult person.* Her state of mind can be likened
to a pressure cooker with a stuck gauge. When the explosion
comes it will be a big one. And everyone will lose.

Is she stupid, enraged, maddened? Is it justified, overreactive,
off the wall? What are the facts and can they be agreed upon by
the disputing parties? Not likely! Probably both are making false
assumptions. Has the vitriolic person lost sight of her objectives?
Completely! Has she considered her needs (to say nothing of the
needs of others)? Of course not, or she might have realized that

she is looking not for vengeance but for love and belonging or safety and security.

Suppose just for purposes of speculation that somehow this moment passes; will she soon do a rerun? Is she really *that* difficult? Can you both, after the moment passes, agree on guidelines for arguing that would prevent a recurrence? Such a discussion would be helpful in pinpointing procedures within which feelings could legitimately be expressed.

How to Cope with the Pressure Cooker

There will be circumstances when nothing you do will change the situation. Your difficult person is too unpredictable for you to hope for a negotiated change. Adjust your expectations when you have dealings with such a personality. If you know it's just a matter of time until the next blowout, gear your thinking to your own behavior: What is least likely to add fuel to the fire and most likely to limit the emotional damage to yourself?

Don't personalize. An explosive boss can cause a lot of stress. You never know when the next outbreak is coming. On the other hand, you can protect your self-esteem by reminding yourself that the tantrum is a matter of style for him, and doesn't indicate a particular antagonism toward you. He probably persists because explosions always get results for him, and so he is not likely to change. Your negotiating problem is to stand up to him without upping the ante. Adopt good eye contact and a firm stance. Calmly allow him to wind down before you speak, and then deal in unemotional facts on a corrective basis. "What would you like me to do to correct the error and when do you want the project completed?"

How to Deal with a Personal Attack

At a formal negotiation, anger may be used as a technique to intimidate, to get you to lower your sights, to force a quick settlement. If it comes as a direct attack on you, no matter what you're feeling, whether it be fury, fear or humiliation, don't buckle. You must let it be known that you won't be intimidated nor will you deal with the situation emotionally. You can acknowledge the problem and arrange to discuss it later when heads are cooler and facts, separate from personalities, can be presented by both parties. Yellers and screamers lose their advantage if they can't

force your action *on the spot*. If you can exercise some control
over timing, you can offset any advantage they may have hoped
to gain by the tirade.

The Bully

The bully establishes a relationship in which he or she feels
confident of getting acquiescence from you. An intimidation script
is set into action and your response is to comply. How can you
blame behavior that has such a predictable outcome? The bully
has found a weak spot and you can bet it will be exploited. He
or she is negotiating, perhaps without even knowing it. And you
are reacting *without* negotiating if you don't recognize the tactics
and do something to counter them.

Face Yourself

Recognize what's going on. Threats or abuse are hounding you
out of the negotiation process.

   Whether you encounter the bully at work or on the home
front, ask yourself:

• Do I show nonverbally or by my demeanor that I'm rattled and
   about to react on cue?
• Am I frightened or just locked into a habit pattern?
• Am I judging each situation on its merits? Sometimes a com-
   mand may have validity, even if it is issued in an overbearing
   manner. If I'm intent on checking my automatic responses, these
   logical demands are not the ones to take a stand on.
• What type of climate do I want to create? Calm? Competent?
   Cooperative? Nonjudgmental?
• Am I ascribing more power to the bully than he actually has?
• Is he this way with everybody?
• Does he have redeeming qualities?
• Is he vulnerable, insecure, a victim of being bullied himself?
• And, what will happen if I say no?

Turn the Bully Around

The bully has found that, with some people, his behavior gets
results. But take a look at him with those people he *can't* manipulate and it's like looking at a different person. He's respectful,
doesn't make unreasonable or excessive demands, and doesn't

try to intimidate. Why? Because the people he respects wouldn't submit to his bullying stance. Because they have demanded a different relationship, they have established one based on reason.

In negotiating with a bully:

- Don't show weakness by gesture or speech.
- Don't back down when he applies more psychological pressure.
- Be absolutely clear on your objectives.
- Maintain a calm, interested, friendly climate even if you're seething.
- Stick to the issues.
- As the relationship changes for the better between you, don't make him feel he's lost in the deal.
- Rather, continue to negotiate in this new fashion. If you gloat, do it internally.

We've all seen movies in which the little kid stands up to the bully, after which they become fast friends who thoroughly respect each other.

You may find something to admire in this former bully once you're no longer "it."

The Liar

We all know that lying is a matter of perception as well as a matter of degree. When asked if he had heard that a mutual friend was on the brink of a marital split because of a lurid sexual escapade, my husband denied having any information to confirm such a damaging rumor. He was lying to protect a friend.

Arriving at a restaurant twenty minutes late, I lied about the crosstown traffic instead of admitting I got a late start. I did it both as an apology and to excuse myself.

In neither of these instances did lying hurt anyone and therefore it need not be seen in a pejorative light.

However, when the input it gives affects your course of action, a lie can create havoc. When I asked Edna in the market research department if our new product had been completed, she said, "Absolutely. No problem. Trust me! All taken care of." I believed her, but she was lying. Her lying has serious ramifications and it makes her a difficult person to negotiate with. In this instance, my prestige was on the line, and I should have recognized her meta-talk. "Trust me" is a phrase that should send out

the signal, "Beware!" But somehow it slipped by and I subsequently spent many sleepless nights before I got the project squared
away.

How to Cope with the Liar

It is not easy to identify a skilled liar before the damage has been
done, but there are clues you can look for.

• Listen for ambiguities in the message.
• Ask for clarification of facts. If the explanation is less than
  scrupulous, press further.
• Watch for evasions, like an attempt to sidetrack your question
  or turn your attention to a different point.
• Learn to recognize telltale signs:
    change in tone of voice; change in pattern (she usually sends
    her report by inter-office mail; why the sudden insistence in
    handing it directly to your superior?); nonverbal signals (a
    prominent political figure in the Watergate debacle answered
    each query of the Congressional committee without hesita-
    tion; as it turned out, whenever he coughed prior to an-
    swering, the answer was a lie).
• If you have the time, investigate reputation.

Can you negotiate with the liar? I don't mean your run-of-
the-mill name dropper or social climber who exaggerates the truth
to enhance his own image. Nor do I mean the person who will
lie occasionally to protect himself or someone else. I have in mind
the person who lies with no guilt, on the spur of the moment, to
manipulate, seduce or impress, or to gain monetary or political
favors.

The fact is that once involved with such a person in business
or in a personal relationship, you have no recourse but to negotiate
skillfully and carefully in order to complete the transaction and
extricate yourself. Later you can decide whether or not to deal
with the same liar again.

While you're in the situation:
• keep the climate positive;
• check your facts;
• check your assumptions;
• set up a review system;
• isolate needs and use them as the basis for a resolution;
• follow through on details along the way;

- be persistent in seeking progress reports;
- leave nothing to chance;
- operate independent of trust;
- think ahead to other sources, manufacturers, etc.;
- change levels in your thinking to gain a new viewpoint;
- start figuring your "out" if you can't bring it all together.

When dealing with a chronic liar, it is more important to focus on the negotiation process itself rather than on the questionable character of the person. It does no good to place such a person in a defensive position. If you try to make him feel guilty, only more lies will result. Rather, keep your objectives at the forefront. Let the liar save face while you adopt techniques such as those stated above. That way you stand a better chance of achieving your goals.

The Irritating Person

Most of us think that people who irritate us are difficult to deal with. But it is a mistake to identify our own reaction to personality quirks and problems with the character of the other person. If someone irritates you because he has a boastful stance or a booming voice, because he taps his pencil, because she is too apologetic—name your own variety—it does not necessarily mean that negotiation will be difficult. It does mean that you will have to come to terms with your reaction to that person. You can find the means within the negotiating process. More than likely it's in the realm of self-negotiation that the problem will be resolved. After all, the offending person is not necessarily aware of the effect his actions have on you, although he might recognize, from observing your nonverbals, that something is amiss. In this instance, you need to clarify in your own mind why the behavior annoys you so much and whether you can overlook it. You had better come to some reconciliation with your own attitudes. The onus is on you, since it's unrealistic to expect the other party to change simply to accommodate you.

It is *you* who must make the adjustment. If your self-negotiation leads you to see that it is too hazardous to confront the other person, you need do nothing more than resort to devices like counting to ten when the tapping starts again. If you feel you must clear the air, be sensitive to what is at stake for the opposing party—his image! You're treading on dangerous ground. Consider the steps you're planning to take as if *you* were the one on the receiving end. Viewed from that perspective, you can foresee the hurt or embarrassment that may occur and make certain that you include methods of saving face in your plan.

Pay attention to your nonverbals. An honest self-analysis may reveal that you have been giving silent signals of disapproval calculated to enlist sympathy from onlookers. Rolling your eyes upward, tilting away from a speaker, foot wiggling, disparaging mouth movements are only a few signals that express annoyance. Surely these are done for effect, to gain attention in some way, to convey an attitude. To whom? Against whom? This is a nonproductive, unfair way of acting and one that you can correct immediately, once you've recognized what you're doing. If you have something to say, say it diplomatically, but say it. If you act it out, people will respect you less, not more. And you probably won't like yourself as well when you recognize what you're doing.

A Final Word

When a negotiation is taking place, even if you find yourself confronting the most difficult of people, you can't just kick over the traces. You must try to maximize your chances for arriving at a settlement satisfactory for everyone involved.

If you finally determine that it's impossible to bring the negotiation to an optimum resolution, you still have to work your way out of it in the most graceful and beneficial way possible. Impulsive moves dictated by emotions will only net you heartache.

Recognize from the very beginning with whom you are negotiating—the other person, but also yourself. Can you see that dealing with yourself may be the more difficult negotiation but ultimately the more important one?

"Impossible" negotiations are negotiations nonetheless. We can't abdicate from them or allow ourselves the mindset that closes us off from the negotiation process. When a situation is too difficult, we may be tempted to abandon the attempt altogether. At such times, remember and recognize the possibilities of change. For one thing, time changes everything. Levels too can be changed, which brings in other people and other circumstances.

In a bad negotiation one can feel like a captive. This is often true of a bitter matrimonial situation involving children. Patient negotiating is the alternative to bitter acrimony. When we opt to view a difficult situation as a negotiation rather than an insoluble problem we're being pragmatic, not merely benevolent. Take the long-range view. If you keep negotiation channels open you are likely to find a mutually advantageous outcome in time.

SEVEN

Negotiating Personal Relationships

The Need for Renegotiation as Time Goes On

Most relationships exist within the framework of unwritten rules that derive legitimacy simply from usage. Roles are assumed because they fill a need. The deferring wife may need the protection and security she gets from a dominating husband. A henpecked husband may need the annoying, but caring, attention he derives from his badgering mate. A child may go out of his way to provoke a parent's punishment in a bid for otherwise unattainable attention. A mate may allow discovery of an indiscretion to ensure the punishment that will expiate guilt. A couple may opt for equal roles within the relationship and establish a rigid rather than loving agenda.

And so, relationships take on a shape of their own and the players assume their roles as surely as if they were actors in a long-running play. But no play runs forever, no matter how successful. And no one remains the same no matter how idyllic the situation, no matter how well suited to the role. As people change, so must the relationship. If a couple keeps each other aware of the new developments in their beliefs, interests, feelings and the like, they may well enhance their lives, adding color and texture to everyday existence. But if this ongoing dialogue is not part of the scheme, trouble looms. It's not fair after ten years of marching to one tune to announce suddenly that you've had it, that you will no longer stand for_____, and you expect a change in_____, and your partner had better_____, and furthermore_____!

Even if the other party has been a sadistic oppressor, if you never before complained, how could he know that anything was amiss? Naturally he would prefer to keep things as they are. Why would he want to change if he is calling the shots? He might say, "Listen, this negotiation was concluded long ago and I'm acting out the agreed-upon settlement!" And you must admit that he'd be correct in stating the case that way. *He* doesn't have the problem. *You* do, and you have to find the means to renegotiate the deal. It is a much more sensitive task to restructure a relationship than it is to start from scratch with a new one. You can bet this is a long procedure, and a taxing one with many roadblocks, so you're in for a rocky time.

It's best to recognize that change implies at least temporary upheaval and the dangerous possibility of open rupture. If you want to alter the boundaries of a relationship approach it as a negotiation without an end, an ongoing encounter in which change will alternate with achieved plateaus after which more change will be forthcoming. The periods of status quo along the way are times for consolidating changes, incorporating them into your nervous system, making them a part of your way of being, before tackling the next step.

During periods when emotions erupt, it is very important to keep the negotiation map in focus so you have some specific guidelines to hold on to. Some key words are also of value:

- Process world—everything changes.
- Objectives—review quickly.
- Needs—assess yours and theirs.
- Climate—keep it positive.
- Assumptions—keep checking for validity.
- Strategy—check against the possibility of damaging the more important element of climate.

When passion threatens to overrule your judgment, these catch phrases will tell you whether you're wandering off course and need to adjust your heading.

Parent and Child

Negotiate with my child? We can just hear you saying, "What are these women talking about? I am the parent, I am the authority figure, and I make the rules." But no matter how benign your intentions, if your child regards your authority as power and experiences your strictures as a win/lose situation, with himself the loser, he will likely look for ways to break the rules. When this happens all the time, or in a crucial aspect of his life, the relationship may suffer irrevocably.

My friend Jane's fifteen-year-old daughter got to know some punk rock musicians, thus achieving instant status in her peer group. She regularly met them at an all-night disco in a dubious neighborhood, beginning her evenings at eleven when the disco opened. She became particularly friendly with one boy and a romance seemed inevitable. Her parents were horrified.

If you're wondering why the parents, intelligent and caring people, didn't put an immediate halt to the activities, the answer is they tried and couldn't. Nothing they tried did the trick! She refused to stop going. She refused to give up her friends.

"You're involved in negotiation, here's one for you," Jane said as she put the problem on the table. "I'm at my wit's end." So, together, we took a fresh look and planned our strategy.

In order to alleviate her own fears, this mother had unsuccessfully sought to gain control: to force the girl to give up her friends and to control her time and how she spent it. These two objectives were not realistic, so we tried to expand the scope of what she hoped to achieve.

• Learn what she could about what was going on.
• Keep informed through open communication.
• Make sure that schoolwork was up to par.
• Avoid alienation.

Suddenly, Jane realized that her knowledge was minimal. She feared for her daughter's safety but she was making assumptions about the actual circumstances that had never been tested against reality. She also assumed—falsely, as it turned out—that her daughter would resent it if her mother visited the disco and met her new friends. Jane had never even considered inviting these friends to her home so she could get to know them firsthand. She began to see that it might be possible to fulfill her own needs and those of her daughter.

JANE'S NEEDS

- Safety for her daughter.
- Love and belonging; maintain mother/daughter relationship.
- Know and understand what was really going on.

DAUGHTER'S NEEDS

- Love and belonging; of both friend and parents.
- Esteem gained from association with this group of people.

While safety was a primary concern on the part of the mother it wasn't even an issue for the girl! Whether right or wrong, she perceived no danger.

Before planning a strategy, Jane and I reviewed the area of climate and the importance of keeping it positive. Rather than respond with anger when taunted or treated with disrespect, she would have to act in a positive manner so that the negotiation would not be destroyed by an escalation of heated emotions.

We then worked out the following strategy:

- *Forbearance*. Wait it out without passing judgment until her own understanding of the situation had improved and perhaps changed.
- *Reversal*. Instead of condemning the scene because of preconceived opinions about "those kinds of people," she would open herself to sharing the experience. Move from open disapproval to an inquiring mode.
- *Participation*. Go to the disco and observe it before making a judgment.
- *Changing levels*. Look at the situation not only from the vantage point of parenthood, but from the social and moral point of view of her daughter.

I spoke to Jane after her evening at the disco. Her daughter had been very pleased that she came and Jane, in turn, found the scene, if not to her liking, less frightening and not as garish as she had expected. The rock group were talented, serious musicians and she came away with a different perspective. The new boyfriend is now a frequent visitor at the house and is well liked by the family.

Don't misunderstand me. Jane would much prefer that this whole association had never taken place. These aren't the people she would choose as her daughter's friends. I reminded her of the "banana principle." Time changes everything. The banana you put in your pocket today will be substantially different next month. You can't control or predict what adventurous changes will occur in a young life. But meanwhile, the family relationship is intact, and everyone is the better for having negotiated the issue so skillfully.

This situation was saved from escalating into a knockdown, drag-out fight, the outcome of which would have been very painful to all participants. In approaching it as a negotiation, Jane avoided being locked into a position diametrically opposed to the position her daughter had adopted. The actions she took in withholding judgment while seeking more knowledge also allowed the girl to loosen her own rigid stand, but with ego intact.

Because Jane dared to ascertain whether her assumptions were in line with the facts, she did not let inertia move her inexorably into a no-win situation. But what if things had not worked out so well? What if Jane's initial negative reaction had been confirmed by direct investigation, if she had found the situation posed a direct threat to her daughter's safety? A subsequent negotiation would then have had to take place and her accumulated data would have been the basis for determining how to go about it.

If her effort to discuss the situation with her daughter was rejected she might have changed levels and enlisted another person (adult or peer whom her daughter trusted) to present her point of view.

If all her efforts to negotiate reasonably were unsuccessful, she would have had to consider a different type of negotiation, using more force. She might even have had to endanger the climate by using strong-arm tactics.
- Discourage his visits to the home.
- Get in touch with his parents to discuss the problem.
- Bribe him.
- Send the daughter to visit a relative.
- Threaten to contact his agent, posing a threat to his career.
- Report (or threaten to report) the discotheque to the license bureau, informing them that underage people are patronizing the establishment.

In planning strategy, the above severe tactics would have to be considered, even if you never plan to use them. Just considering them would make you realize the high risk involved in their use. Any one of them would be a last resort for those extreme instances when nothing else is working.

When you put someone at high risk, you can't anticipate the reaction. Think of it this way; if you fulfill people's needs, they are more likely to cooperate with you. If, on the other hand, you thwart their needs, who knows what measures they'll take to resist you?

If Jane had had to use such pressure in this case, she might have made an enemy of her daughter or precipitated an elopement.

In negotiating personal relationships where emotions very often dictate action, consider working *for* the needs and creating a positive climate as ultimately the best strategy.

Negotiating with Experts

Women often complain that when they consult a male doctor they are given short shrift. The professional condescends, refusing to give details of their illness or the medicine that's supposed to cure it. Questions are ignored; if the woman patient wants to discuss an alternative treatment, her probing is taken as criticism.

If she consults a lawyer, similar problems emerge. His attitude may be that she shouldn't worry about a thing, he'll take care of all the details, even as she is asking for information that will prepare her to participate more fully.

If you get this kind of treatment from someone you're paying to represent you, the first thing to remember is that you do not have to acquiesce. You can make it clear that you intend to participate in the decision-making process and that he must therefore be willing to explain things to your satisfaction.

In any case, you must do some fact finding of your own in order to evaluate what he tells you.

- Is his expertise, in fact, sufficient for your purposes?
- What is his point of view? Is it compatible with your own?
- Are you clear in your own mind about what you want to know?
- It is helpful to prepare questions in advance. In questioning him, have you indicated sufficiently that you are interested in hearing the alternatives?
- Can he direct you to the literature or specific associations formed

to disseminate information about your problem?

As in any negotiation, we must be aware of the needs of our expert and act to satisfy them as well as our own.

Before your appointment:

- Cue him that you need a few minutes extra to discuss your case and are willing to pay for the time.
- Figure out exactly what you need to know.
- Make a list of your questions.

At your meeting:

- Be terse.
- Make quick notes as he talks.
- Make sure your questions are information-seeking and avoid a cross-examination style.

Above all, remember when dealing with experts that this is a negotiation in which you are at least an equal—indeed, the primary party. The expert needs *you* for information and guidance just as much as you need him.

A Divorce

Of all the personal relationships which must be negotiated, the breakup of a marriage is usually one of the most difficult in which to maintain a win/win attitude. Yet it is in just such a negotiation, particularly when there are children involved, that it is most important to adhere to this philosophy. When emotions are running high, it sometimes seems impossible to care about the consequences, but the consequences of this negotiation will affect everyone for the rest of their lives. It is well to remember that.

Subject Matter

Make certain first that divorce is indeed the subject. If one party wants a divorce and the other wants a positive change in the relationship, your first negotiation in this instance will be to agree on the subject matter.

Objectives

The more you can expand them realistically, the better your chance for fulfilling them. It's time to take pencil and paper in hand and make a list of your objectives.

- End the marriage.

- Build the criteria for a future relationship. What do you want it to be one year, five years, twenty years down the road?
- Make provision for ancillary relationships to continue, with in-laws and friends.
- Make financial arrangements that provide for various contingencies on the part of both spouses. Are they acceptable? Can they be changed?

Existence of children, and providing for them, may affect your position. Bitterness, hard feelings and strong emotion are present; the desire to blame the other spouse may have to be kept in check in order to create equitable, long-range solutions of problems affecting the offspring.

The Issues

There will be many: Who should pay legal fees; how the furniture should be divided; whether to keep the cottage at Fire Island; the type of schooling the children should have; joint custody as opposed to visitation rights.

Some issues on an agenda—custody, for instance—are more serious than others. You might decide to make a concession on the furniture and the summer cottage in order to encourage agreement on a larger issue.

Positions

It is particularly important not to get frozen into positions that can deadlock the negotiation. While you may take a position of initial intransigence on *all* the issues in an effort to lower the other person's expectations, you should realize that rigidity may damage the climate irretrievably and force your opponent to hang tough on all *his* positions. With such polarization, negotiating can come to a halt.

Realistically, positions change during the give-and-take. If you relinquish your position of retaining all the furniture, for instance, your husband may cooperate in the schooling plans. Each agreement narrows the issues and brings you closer to a workable settlement.

Fact Finding

Once again it's time to make a list, which may include the following:

- A determination of the financial picture: his bank account, your bank account, and joint holdings in cash, investments, property, etc.
- You don't have concrete evidence of his other holdings but you suspect they exist.
- He has rented living quarters that will comfortably accommodate the children for visits.
- The cost of legal fees will exceed $30,000.
- The cost of training to update the skills you need to become self-supporting is $5,000.
- The time he has available to spend with the children is limited.

Examine the facts you've arrived at to check which are assumptions. For instance, you *assume* he has other holdings about which you know nothing. You are also making an *assumption* about his available time. These are not facts and should be distinguished from them.

Needs

- To survive. Literally, to find the emotional and financial means to carry you through this difficult time with the least trauma to the children.
- To feel loved and needed and, conversely, to give up hating your ex-mate.
- To occupy yourself in satisfying work to begin regaining self-esteem.
- To be self-sufficient and know your own strength.

Your needs seem voracious but in listing them they fall into a natural hierarchy. Your esteem needs are not a primary concern if you are genuinely worried about feeding and clothing your children. As the means to satisfy the most basic needs become apparent, other needs such as esteem and self-actualization emerge. First things first!

Climate

One of the ironies of life is that the behavior that will reward you most is often the opposite of the way you're tempted to act. A divorce negotiation is a prime example of a situation so imbued with strong feelings that objectivity is hard to maintain. Parties to a divorce often act against their own best interests, only to generate even more bad feeling. Achieving a workable arrangement is very difficult when passion is calling the action.

He says: She makes it difficult to see the kids. She wants to rob me blind.

She says: He doesn't care what happens to me. He walked out and I'll make him pay.

What both are really saying is: I'm furious; I'm hurt; I don't know what to do, but I want to retaliate.

Think "map." Go through the negotiation process; when you reach "climate," realize that in a negotiation (as opposed to a knock-down-drag-out fight), it is your responsibility to:

- Pause long enough to choose a rational response.
- Restrain yourself from being goaded into a hostile reaction.
- Calculate your exchanges to encourage cooperative dialogue.
- Don't react to an effort to intimidate you by backing down.
- Hold your ground, *without being inflammatory*.

In short, when confronted with a negative climate, respond with one that is positive. Don't be a partner in tearing the negotiation apart!

Strategy

Plan your strategy around those ploys that will help you and your ex-mate reach a settlement. That means eliminating the tactics most likely to be resented. Threatening and making the other party jealous, fearful, suspicious or wary do not resolve the situation.

- Forbearance is valuable. It gains time and halts the escalation.
- An agent with limited authority (friend, counselor, lawyer) can present your positions if speaking directly is too heated.
- Change levels. Think of the proceedings from the point of view of the children. Think of how the extended family can act as a support system.

Stringent ploys such as feinting, withdrawal, surprise and deadlines may sometimes seem expedient, but if you use them be prepared for the backfire. One woman used the tactic of withdrawal, hoping to increase the size of her alimony as the price for reinstating the negotiation. But her husband had had it, and what could have been resolved through mediation went to trial, where she was awarded less support than what had originally been offered.

In another case, an irate husband used a surprise tactic. He produced bills for several expensive items his wife had purchased just prior to their separation, hoping to persuade her to lower her demands. Instead she countered with a surprise of her own—the bill for a mink coat he had purchased for another woman.

Tactics used to hurt or frighten often end up in dirty tricks. Even if one side wins a skirmish, everyone tends to lose the war.

In most negotiations, particularly in the instance of divorce, if you think of what the situation will be next year, or five years from now, a different perspective is gained. Seeing things as a process helps to remind you that your relationship is not ended with a divorce decree, especially if children are involved. The need for finding an amicable method for dealing with each other remains acute.

Time changes everything, both fact and circumstances. A major fault with most difficult negotiations is impatience. We want quick results. So many people are not prepared to let the factor of time heal a wound. All of us who have suffered the loss of a loved one and thought we could never recover from the loss know that the passing of time works miracles on the emotions. So it should be in a matrimonial negotiation. The outcome should strive to satisfy each person's needs. If one party feels like a loser, he or she will try to even the score.

Negotiating with the Elderly

In our age of specialization, even skilled negotiators often find themselves ill at ease when their opponent is someone "different" from those with whom they are accustomed to negotiate. Virtually any group can cause this unease: men, women, minority groups, the rich, the poor, borrowers or lenders. Unfortunately, when dealing with the elderly, even those we are familiar with, it sometimes seems as if we're in a foreign country.

Possibly the greatest impediment to communication and, therefore, negotiation with the elderly are assumptions and prejudices about age and aging, such as:

• They can't judge what is best for them.
• They are no longer a business asset.
• They require special consideration which is not feasible to give.
• They are difficult.

So when dealing with "the elderly" it is important to examine our feelings carefully and decide whether they are in tune with the reality. Chronological age is not necessarily identical with emotional and physical aging. However, when changes take place in body and mind that make independent functioning difficult, the elderly may require our help and direction, and we may be presented with a negotiating situation that can be troubling for both parties involved.

The importance of preparation prior to any negotiation cannot be overstated. In dealing with the elderly this fact is particularly significant. A negotiation planning checklist helps us to consider important items. The example which follows outlines a negotiation with an elderly person regarding the taking of medicine.

Negotiation Preparation Checklist

SUBJECT MATTER
- How and when medicine is to be taken.

OBJECTIVE
- Maximum: Make her completely responsible for taking own medicine.
- Minimum: Agree to remind her by telephone on a regular basis.

FACT FINDING
- Learn as much as I can about other party's life, experiences, likes, dislikes and viewpoints.
- Understand present physical condition, with emphasis on physical infirmities.
- Know medicines and drugs taken, their effect, and to what degree they may enhance or limit capacities.
- Status of present social life or lack thereof.
- Agencies that may be helpful.

ISSUES
- Isolate points of disagreement to be negotiated: I want her to be responsible for taking her own medicine; she refuses to take responsibility for taking medicine.

POSITION
- Alternative stands I might take on issues, giving me flexibility of action.
    I will not assume any responsibility.
    I will not make calls to remind her.
    I'm willing to spot-check.

I'll share responsibility with a relative.

I'll do it on a regular basis.

NEEDS INVOLVED

- I need to assure myself that the medicine is taken.
- I am too busy to give it to her myself.
- I need to free myself from guilt in regard to this.

STRATEGY

- Fait accompli: Assume she will take medicine to force her hand in accepting responsibility.
- Association: Point out to her that people she admires assume this responsibility, encouraging her to do likewise.
- Any other strategy I can use effectively.

Having examined the elements, we have arrived at a clearer picture of what is involved and some of the alternatives available. But our preparation is far from complete, for we have only made this calculation from our own point of view. We have not yet tried to examine each element from the elderly person's point of view. To do so we must go through our checklist once more. It may point the way to a solution. For instance, in trying to understand this person's needs, we may discover that what is really being asked for is evidence of love and belonging and that the taking of medicine is not really the issue at all. It may be the phone call, not the reminder, which she needs. If we can satisfy this need for love and belonging, we can conclude our negotiation successfully, the outcome will be beneficial to both parties, and each will work hard to keep it going.

Long-Term Relationships

Close long-term associations often run into difficulty. Expectations remain the same, even in the face of evident changes taking place. Habit and complacency often keep us from examining old assumptions to check whether they still have validity. We push from our minds the fact that everything changes over time. This can be particularly true in a marriage.

A Marriage Renegotiation

Jeff had no objection to Tania's going back to work part-time when the children were all in school, as long as *his* life didn't change substantially. He even agreed to drop the kids at school in the morning. He balked, however, at some of Tania's growing desire for independence. Why did she want her own bank account after all these years of joint banking? And when he bought some investment property (a small apartment house with eight tenants), he positively sputtered at her request that she appear on the deed as co-owner.

Tania was surprised. Although Jeff had always handled their finances, paying most of the bills and keeping the records, he had also always been generous with money and had never questioned her decisions on purchases. She had not expected him to refuse this new wish of hers for financial independence.

Well, she thought, this is a first. I guess we're going to have to talk about the *subject* of money. She did a quick review of her *objectives*. She wanted to use some of the money she earned for personal and family projects that they might not indulge in, and possibly build a nest egg for emergencies. And, in case anything happened to Jeff, she wanted some financial assets of her own. She realized that Jeff's objective was to maintain control of an area where he was used to making or endorsing all decisions.

What *needs* were involved for each of them? Hers were clear. A greater sense of financial security and a feeling of financial independence which would give her greater self-esteem. At first she could not understand what needs Jeff was trying to satisfy by his opposition, but she realized that he must feel threatened in some way. As they talked, it became clear that he saw her desire for independence as signaling less commitment to the marriage (an *assumption* on his part which was not true).

Since she had not lost her temper and she could genuinely reassure him that she loved him, she was able to maintain a *climate* that fostered trust and goodwill and allowed for a rational and open exchange. Though Jeff started out with, "I can't see what you need any of this for," he was finally willing to accept Tania's desire for independence, with a surprise caveat. "If you really want your name on a piece of property, then you ought to be able to manage it. You can be the joint owner if you'll take on the responsibility of running it."

She gulped. "What does that entail?" (A *fact finding* question within the negotiation.)

"Collecting rents, paying bills, handling complaints, getting repairs made, sometimes appealing tax assessments. There will have to be some renovation in the building, and you'll have to deal with the contractor and the workmen."

"Do you think I can do it?" (A question she might not have asked if his approach had not become sympathetic.)

"I know you can." Jeff was growing positively enthusiastic. "And I think it's a terrific idea. Since you're working part-time, you have more time than I do." He promised he would always be available for advice.

So it was agreed. But Jeff still couldn't understand why she needed a bank account of her own, and he finally convinced her that since he always consulted her about any large expenditures, it was only fair that she should do the same, and that both their earnings should go into the same pot.

While neither one of them got exactly what they had originally had in mind, both of them were excited by the results of this negotiation. Tania ended up with not only greater financial independence, but with a responsibility which would increase her ability and skill, and Jeff achieved some needed space in an overburdened work schedule. While maintaining the atmosphere of love and respect which had characterized their marriage, they had entered into a somewhat altered relationship which held possibilities for renewed interest and growth.

In fact, it was the kind of ideal negotiation in which both parties won pieces of a larger pie.

Salvaging an Old Friendship

Sometimes change occurs in an increasingly dramatic way that makes you wonder if a relationship will be able to last. I couldn't understand the change in my friend Midge. I had been noting incidents in which she would switch from friendliness to overt hostility in a minute. When her anger toward me over a returned blouse that hadn't been ironed properly erupted at a party, I was furious at this public humiliation, even while realizing that the issue she had chosen as a pretext was totally out of proportion. I'd had it. Such was my first reaction. Then I did a mental click into a few familiar words: objectives, needs, assumptions, fact finding, climate.

OBJECTIVE
Maintain the friendship at all costs.

NEEDS

What the devil did she need from me? Attention? A scapegoat? Someone with the fortitude to probe further?

ASSUMPTIONS

I had already made the erroneous assumption that her anger was directed at me. I examined that more closely.

FACT FINDING

Revealed that she felt close enough to me to vent a fury she didn't herself understand. Seeking some rational pattern in her actions, I began to see a correlation between anger and alcohol, after which the "facts" unfolded—to uncover a desperate alcoholic.

CLIMATE

I made the decision to keep it positive no matter how negative her actions toward me became.

She really needed a friend. Self-negotiating and the reminder of those few key words allowed me to be one. We both grew from the experience. She's fine and the friendship endures.

Negotiating Your Mood

Recently I woke up in the doldrums with that low feeling that announces, "This is going to be a bummer of a day. I wish I didn't have to join it!" There were no precipitating events that I could blame, although ongoing problems varying in severity might have accounted for it. Rather than merely hoping it would eventually go away, I decided to test a hypothesis: that I could negotiate with myself to change my mood. I've thought and rethought the negotiation process so often that it's truly a part of my nervous system, so much so that I can simulate the map in my mind's eye without putting pen to paper.

In attempting to negotiate with myself over the issue of mood, I focused on several elements which are particularly relevant to this type of negotiation: objectives, fact finding, needs, climate and strategy.

OBJECTIVES

• Get over the depression.
• Function productively.

FACT FINDING

• Was today different from any other day?
• In what verifiable way?

- What if anything did I do to bring on the mood?

NEEDS

- It was clear that my immediate needs fell into the areas of love and belonging, self-esteem, and maybe a little self-actualization. There were no serious crises with regard to my safety and security, and certainly no life-threatening situation. In effect, I needed a boost, a shot in the arm, something to raise my morale—and I would have to create it!

CLIMATE

- To change the gloom and doom climate I found myself in, I could swing the following guns into action:

    Physical activities and diversions: flowers, colored clothing, going out to lunch, exercise.

    Nonverbals: correct depressed attitudes such as slouching, lowered head, low voice, nervous gestures.

    Communication with others: even if forced, be friendly, polite, speak in a clear voice, don't be tentative.

STRATEGY

- Change levels: avoid isolating myself, go to a meeting.
- Association: touch base with a friend.
- Escalate activities: structure the day, include several pleasant breaks, make evening plans.

    The very act of mentally going through the process of self-negotiation gave me energy. I don't know how else to explain the slight surge that got me over the initial inertia and put me into an action mode. I began to see my feelings in clearer terms and set in motion a plan of action to supersede the depression of the moment. It was as if the change had already taken place in my mind. My initial feeling of floating gloom didn't disappear but it lessened—almost immediately!

    We already have discussed the fact that time alters everything. Moods change over time, for better or worse and back again, whether we do something to alter them or not. And so it would have been with me. But this instance was different. I didn't wait for the change. By referring to the elements of the negotiation process I was able to alter my mood sooner. The reason for my depression that morning was never clear, and probably was unimportant. I was just grateful to be able to dispel the mood quickly and hopeful that the same type of exercise would allow me to repeat the quickened relief another time.

But suppose the gloom had been precipitated by a specific and serious happening; a death in the family, an argument that resulted in a serious breach with someone I love, a bitterness born of betrayal by a trusted friend?

Will self-negotiation serve well in an instance of such over-powering emotion? What should the expectations be?

It's worth a try! Identifying needs, defining objectives for the future, confronting the fact of the grief, working to create a more cheerful climate; these are all positive cognitive actions. In a state of loneliness and self-isolation, however, such a solitary endeavor may not be enough. If too deeply immersed in a serious dilemma, such solitary analysis may not give the perspective you need to start moving on. You need to talk to a wise friend, or perhaps a counselor who is emotionally removed from the situation and who can lead you to insights you're not able to come up with by yourself.

In negotiating your mood, recognize you are not "an island, entire of itself." Seek whatever help you may need to reach a successful conclusion.

How to Use the Map to Resuscitate a Negotiation

How do you resuscitate a negotiation that is falling apart because of personality differences? It's likely that you have been in a situation in which:

- You can't find out what the other side wants or needs.
- You can't break through their suspicion and hostility.
- They present roadblocks that preclude any settlement.

To complicate matters, you know that in the future you're going to be negotiating with this person whether you like it or not.

Place yourself in a scenario that might occur to any of us. The opposition has been wary from the start. Their stance is measured, possibly hostile, and nothing seems to ease matters. In response you're starting to indulge in verbal barbs and de-signing a strategy to show that you won't be pushed around. You recognize that things are falling apart but what do you do?

First, stop and face yourself. Have you fallen into fixed habits of response that may have more to do with assumptions and expectations than with the objective reality? Do you bear any responsibility for the situation that has developed? What do you really want? Negotiate with yourself.

Then prepare a negotiation in terms of objectives, fact finding, needs and climates to get your thinking started.

In-Laws

Linda found herself in such a deteriorating situation with her mother-in-law. Although she didn't doubt that the woman's intentions were good, she felt that her mother-in-law was interfering with her life and with her methods of raising her children. Her resentment had started to spill over into the marriage. In speaking to her husband she found herself often saying "*your* mother" in a tone which clearly conveyed displeasure. The friction with her husband made it imperative to take some measures, and deciding to apply her negotiating skills to the matter, she drew up a list of objectives, facts and climates.

OBJECTIVES
- Short term:
  Reestablish ongoing contact.
  Make sure her children could see the grandparents regularly.
  End the friction developing between her husband and herself.
  Find joint interests to explore as family activities.
- Long term:
  Maintain cordial relations with her in-laws.
  Find a suitable balance relative to the amount of time spent together.
  Make the family experiences enjoyable events.
  Establish a climate in which any differences of opinion could be explored without rancor.

FACT FINDING
- Exploration of her mother-in-law's feelings disclosed that:
  Her mother-in-law felt pressured by the feeling that she was *supposed* to be so involved.
  She would welcome less frequent but more meaningful experiences.
  She did not wish to interfere.
  She was indeed willing to abide by her daughter-in-law's guidelines.
  She was willing to spend some weekends with the children and give her son and daughter-in-law a holiday.

CLIMATE

- Linda's mother-in-law had a way of expressing herself that had been interpreted as critical but really wasn't. Now the daughter-in-law consciously sought to better the climate by not responding sharply to a supposed barb. Consequently, suspicion and touchiness diminished on both sides and the climate gradually improved. In subsequent discussions they verified that this was the most helpful part of restoring their friendship.

NEEDS

- Individual Needs: The mother-in-law needed to feel loved and needed; the daughter-in-law needed to maintain her privacy. As they sought to fulfill these needs, their increased understanding of each other made it easier to recognize and fulfill their:
- Common Needs: For family get-togethers, for shared responsibilities, for alliance. The outcome was a modus operandi that worked. As it turned out, once the decision to renegotiate was made, the doing wasn't difficult.

EIGHT

Negotiating in the Workplace

The Woman Entrepreneur

There has been a rapid increase in the number of women who own their own businesses. A recent radio report indicates that 25 percent of new businesses are started by women, and so many of them succeed that it demonstrates how quickly women can learn the ropes.

The risks, however, are great, and the anxiety they provoke can be punishing. Why, then, are so many women eager to accept the challenge?

For one thing, the personal satisfactions are substantial: making rules, giving orders, planning strategy, running your own thing. Also, the financial horizons are wider than when working for someone else. Climbing the rungs of a male-dominated corporate ladder is very often difficult for a woman and her monetary sights there may be limited. In many areas of work, salaries are substantially lower than those men command. Jobs that tend to be associated with women workers (teachers, nurses, secretaries, book editors) are on the low paying end. Therefore, going into business for oneself holds the potential for greater financial reward, with all the benefits financial independence brings. As Dr. Penelope Russianoff said, "The more a woman pays her own way, the more self-esteem she has. Financial security goes a long way toward building your inner core of security."*

*Russianoff, Penelope. *Why Do I Think I'm Nothing Without a Man?* (New York: Bantam Books, 1982).

And what a boost to the ego to build a business. Each obstacle surmounted adds to self-confidence, which in turn fuels the operation. A woman entrepreneur is a risk taker; she walks a tightrope without a net, no boss or mentor to pick her up when she falls. Rather than choosing to follow corporate rules and come up through the ranks in a traditional step-by-step fashion, she is ambitious enough to take a flyer, strike out on her own, put herself on the line. Harry Truman's often quoted words, "The buck stops here," apply to her. And it's rough going at the start because there's so much to learn and so many pitfalls along the way. The concerns of a business owner are of a different sort than those of an employee. A corporate woman might worry about how to advance to the next step on the ladder, how to make herself visible, how to use words to get recognition from a superior. A woman running her own business is more likely to be concerned with how to negotiate with a banker for that $150,000 loan she needs to survive, or how to ascertain which supplier she'll get the best price from without sacrificing service. And at least some of the people she has to negotiate with will think they can take advantage of her just because she is a woman.

Before You Decide, Negotiate with Yourself

If you intend to go it alone as a business owner you had better cover all bases in the planning stages. This can be done by a thorough negotiation with yourself to determine whether you're up to taking the risk and, if you go ahead, to maximize the success of a projected venture. Questions to ask yourself are:

- Am I willing to work around the clock, thinking about my problem twenty-four hours a day?
- Am I willing to sacrifice a social life, if necessary?
- What are my family demands that might limit the time I need to start a business?
- Who is going to be affected by my commitment to a business? Even if I prepare physically for children's care, for instance, can I handle the psychological aspects of guilt or anxiety that my absence may produce in me?
- Can I raise the money needed to start?
- Have I considered partners with whom to share the work, risk and profits?
- What expertise do I have: manufacturing knowledge, running

the finances of a business, source of supply, connections, a unique product design, a product for which there is a ready market?

• What is my competition; if there is none, who is likely to jump on the bandwagon to spoil my exclusivity?

• Have I allowed for making the usual number of mistakes before a solid working organization is built? One-third of new businesses fail in the first year.

• Have I built in a financial cushion for survival over lean times? Most new businesses fail because of lack of capital.

• Can I get credit?

• Have I established a working arrangement with a bank?

• What assumptions am I relying on?

• What experts do I need to consult? Am I clear on what I want of them? Good professionals can save much heartache.

• What state is the economy in? Inflation rate, interest rate, tight money, etc. What is it likely to be a year from now? Two years? Ten?

Having truly considered these and other questions, if you're still hot to trot, go to it. You've got the kind of ambition and confidence that an entrepreneur needs.

Negotiating Problems of the New Entrepreneur

For a new owner, negotiating is certainly an ongoing reality— dealing with suppliers, craftsmen, salespeople, employees, government agencies, banks, leases for premises and so on. The number and variety of situations which need negotiating escalate as the enterprise grows and new conditions arise. That there are no pat answers soon becomes apparent. What is critical is a knowledge of the negotiating process. Negotiating skill may come more or less naturally, but it grows with experience until it becomes an integral part of the entrepreneur's mode of operation.

Starting an advertising agency in competitive San Francisco isn't an easy route to travel. I asked Mimi Sheiner about specific negotiating problems she had as a budding entrepreneur. She found it useful to make her first contact with potential clients over the phone. In that way she overcame the disadvantage of looking too young to inspire confidence. She had done her homework and knew enough about her potential clients' needs to persuade them when she called that she understood those needs and knew how to satisfy them. She made it clear that she was eager to establish a long relationship with clients, would put in that extra effort, and her fees would be moderate. (She had done the necessary fact finding to know what the market would bear.)

So impressive were her proposals that face-to-face meetings followed. They may have been surprised at her youth, but she had inspired enough confidence by that time to get the contracts she needed.

Her initial dealings with suppliers were disheartening. She feels that her youth and the fact that she was a woman gave them license to try to take advantage of her inexperience. Fortunately she had apprised herself of the best prices she might expect and insisted on a fair deal. Hers was not a confrontational style. Rather she emphasized the potential for a long relationship, never allowing her anger to interfere with her objective of getting those supplies. After a few such dealings, suppliers agreed that she knew her stuff.

With success, her negotiating has moved into the area of how to expand while at the same time maintaining a personal life. She is looking for a partner now, and that is a whole new area of negotiation. As a first step, she has negotiated with herself and established the following:

NEEDS
• More time for personal life.
• Actively seek more clients.
• Be able to increase support personnel.
• Relieve pressure of doing it all and the anxiety of anticipating a crisis such as illness or unforeseen emergencies.
• A "design" person to complement her major strength, which is conceptual creativity.

OBJECTIVES
• Ideally, to find a working partner, someone with money to invest who will also share in the decision making.
• If she cannot find the right full partner, to work out an initial partial arrangement with the possibility of future greater commitment.

FACT FINDING
• Assessing her own strengths and weaknesses, she determined that the profile of the ideal partner would be: An older person with sales ability, experienced in administration and production.

STRATEGY

• Her strategy for conducting such a search is to cover as wide an area as possible—"blanketing," in our parlance. Tactics include:

Lunch with designers.

Put out the word to everybody that she's looking.

Increase attendance at trade meetings.

Consult a search and recruitment firm on a contingency basis, not a flat fee.

By first negotiating with herself, she has established a plan on which she can now proceed to act. Her future negotiation with a prospective partner will be designed to bring larger benefits to both.

The Woman Executive

Special Problems of the Woman Executive

As we all know, women executives have different problems than their male counterparts. For one thing, the stereotyped images of women many men still hold to puts women at a psychological disadvantage. If a man sees a woman boss as the "mother" or "teacher" telling the child what to do, he may feel that his status is lowered, that his job has been diminished because a woman has been chosen to head the unit. In addition, as more women move up the corporate ladder, they are meeting with an unexpected backlash. Several studies have indicated that when only token numbers of women hold high positions, they are met with goodwill and cooperation on the part of male workers. But a recent study at Wellesley College suggests that as the proportion of women executives increases, so do insults and harassments. "Men begin to fear that they will lose out to women in promotions," says researcher Carol Weiss.*

A real dilemma exists when the number of jobs is thought of as finite. It's not likely that women will go back to the home in droves nor is it probable that their ambition will decrease and they will stop striving for higher positions. Therefore, the only

---

*In "Male Workers and Female Bosses Are Confronting Hard Challenges," by Carole Hymowitz, *Wall Street Journal*, July 16, 1984.

satisfactory solution lies in making a bigger pie, using the best available talent, male and female, to create more jobs, greater production and expanded potential for everyone.

As things now stand, however, women must often find special ways to negotiate with the men they supervise. One woman manager found that several men in her department showed their resentment by ignoring her requests, in effect denying that she had the authority to call the shots. Those who did cooperate with her were teased by the others for playing up to a woman.

To get the situation in hand she organized a weekend session at which problems were discussed in a social setting. Everyone emerged with a better understanding of each other's problems and with a healthier respect all around. How she negotiated the funds for the weekend must have been masterful.

Along with the added stature a management position offers comes the responsibility for giving orders, possibly increasing the workload, or giving criticism for an inferior job. In such instances, explaining the reason for your request will gain cooperation where a curt order won't. Give people sufficient time to prepare themselves for additional tasks, and give all the attention, interest and assistance you can. Don't forget to praise a worker who comes through for you.

When dealing with a recalcitrant male worker, make an effort to get to know him. Pitching in when the workload is heavy will prove your capability. If you give work orders to other people in his presence, their acceptance of your requests will help induce him to accept your authority. If nothing you try abates his defiance, try the direct approach and ask him why he hasn't accepted you. In any case, continue to be task-oriented. Getting the job done is the focus to pursue, not the personalities of the opposing parties.

A recent phone survey by Kane Parsons & Associates Inc. found that a large percentage of women also buy the stereotypical views of women bosses. False notions abound: that men are fairer and more understanding while women are petty, envious, power-mad and too aggressive; that it's more difficult to work for a woman boss because she will be more demanding and focus on every small detail. However, these prejudices quickly fall by the wayside if a woman boss is productive, supportive and efficient.

How Negotiating Skill Can Smooth the Way

An unusual woman who was appointed plant manager is a case in point. She was not only the first woman to hold the position but her meteoric rise through the company had bypassed most of the usual steps. As reported in the *Wall Street Journal* by Carole Hymowitz, she said, "That job had always been held by a man who had come up through the ranks and whose hands were dirtied. So I put myself in the shoes of my staff and thought about how I'd feel if I suddenly got a new boss whom I didn't think was qualified." She asked for their support, acknowledged their expertise in their own jobs, told them that she could offer them something they didn't have—better representation and communication with the higher powers. Their skeptical attitude changed and a fine working relationship was the result.*

People must learn to play office politics. Women have to learn to develop their negotiating and communicating skills. Having the foresight to see the relevance of interoffice relationships will keep you from isolating yourself at a desk, merely completing a task.

Because they feel insecure, some women operate on the assumption that the best defense is a good offense. This might be effective at times, but too often it results in a kind of stridency that sets people's teeth on edge and creates an instant wariness in the other party. It's wise to remember that the start of a negotiation is a period of sizing up, so what you say should have a purpose and you should be able to substantiate it. Striving for effect may create a damaging impression.

The main thing to remember is to be yourself. Approach each situation with an open mind. Don't get hamstrung by a predetermined style that may not be appropriate. You can be soft, strong, inquiring, authoritative or even bitchy; but whatever tack you take should be based on what you perceive as the requirements of that particular negotiation.

The Problem of Doing It All

The biggest problem women have is managing a job while they run a home and bring up children, too. When we speak to women

* *Wall Street Journal*, July 16, 1984.

across the country, this is the overriding concern. It is not an issue
of "whether" but "how" to have it all and do it well.

Fortunately, employers are beginning to offer some help.
Thomas Hoffman, a professor in the School of Management at
the University of Minnesota, says that the use of flextime is on
the rise in American corporations and he expects the trend to
widen as the United States continues its transition from a production to a service economy. Some innovations are:

- Giving workers the option of taking vacation time in small units,
  a few days at a time or afternoons off. (This works better in a
  service industry than on a production line.)
- The retail industry stays open longer hours using shifts of workers with more flexible scheduling.
- A week's work is split by two people. My librarian friend was
  able to convince her school district to institute such a program
  and it worked out wonderfully. Each worker had the time she
  needed to raise a family, they complemented each other by
  dividing the workload along lines that each preferred, and the
  job got done more efficiently.
- On-premises day care for children has been instituted in a few
  companies and is a boon to workers who can't afford expensive
  care and for whom no other avenue exists. In companies which
  do not provide such help, however, a woman must be even more
  creative to get what she needs and deserves.

A Tale of One Woman

Marilyn, a mother of three young children, worked free-lance for
a large publishing firm. As she took on more and more responsibility, the job provided an added dimension to her life that she
cherished. Although she didn't want to increase her hours, she
felt that her status as chief media consultant merited gaining the
health and pension benefits that her free-lance status denied her.
Using the negotiation map, she planned her negotiation as follows:

SUBJECT MATTER

Terms of employment. Her employer agreed that this would be
the item to resolve.

OBJECTIVES

- Become a staff employee, on a part-time basis.
- Increase her salary.

- Convince them to create a new department for her to administer.
- Demonstrate that this new department would increase revenue and thus pay for itself.

In trying to second-guess what her opponents' objectives would be she realized they would want to save money, and thus would be unwilling to commit themselves to added salary or benefits. On the other hand, she believed they wanted to continue a working relationship with her.

- If she couldn't get an absolute commitment for a department, arrange a trial-basis authorization, to become a permanent department if she generated new revenue.

FACT FINDING

She armed herself with knowledge of how such plans worked in other businesses, the exact hours she would be prepared to give, and the time needed to set up the department. She was prepared with charts and figures to substantiate specific proposals for expanding productivity. She would show the additional tasks she had successfully undertaken on her own to demonstrate the ingenuity she would bring to a new endeavor.

She surmised that her employer's fact finding would confirm that she was a productive, innovative worker. They might not, however, be able to confirm factually whether her proposals would be cost effective.

NEEDS

She needed not only the security of an in-house position, but the status the position would bring her, whereas she realized that the employer's needs were for profit and growth. They also needed stable office personnel who worked well together.

ISSUES

For both negotiators they were the same:

- Creation of a new department.
- Putting her on staff.
- Salary.

POSITIONS

- Hers

    They need the new department.

    She needs a new working status and more salary.

- Employer's

    They're happy with the way things are now.

CLIMATES

She might encounter a negative climate on her employer's part, a reluctance to listen to her case, perhaps, or an effort to squelch her proposal by immediate rejection. She would neither be deterred by such an effort nor become defensive and antagonistic. This could turn out to be a multiphased negotiation. By maintaining a positive climate, she might ultimately gain the opportunity to negotiate the details.

STRATEGY

- Hers

    Present overwhelming data to justify her proposal.

    Speak to *the* person with authority to grant her the position, not to an agent with limited authority.

    Association: enlist the aid of powerful allies to speak up for her.

    Surprise: another job offer.

    Limits: statement of how long she will wait if they delay.

- Employer's

    They might forbear, hoping to wear her down.

    They might try to use an agent with limited authority.

    Feinting: they might suggest they have someone else to take her present workload.

    Surprise: they might grant her the department but not staff status.

In trying to figure out her strategies and the possible reactions to each ploy, Marilyn recognized the drawbacks of depending on strategy alone to gain her ends.

PHILOSOPHY

The change she was proposing should bring satisfaction and gain for both parties.

As it turned out, this attitude so permeated the negotiation that her proposal was greeted sympathetically and accepted readily. She gained the benefits she sought.

It was in the planning of the negotiation that Marilyn found the persuasive arguments to pursue and the courage to initiate the process.

Companies and Climates

As reported in *In Search of Excellence*, successful companies create climates among the staff that contribute in large part to their success. Their philosophy dictates respect for the individual. They treat people as adults and make them winners. It doesn't require learned MBAs to create atmosphere. A company does need people who, whether schooled or not, can't understand why a product isn't high quality, why a customer shouldn't get personalized attention and service, why production lags, why a worker's suggestions are ignored. These companies have more faith in workers and feel more responsibility to the customer. They believe in fewer words and more action, rather than in lengthy market studies.*

Have you noticed that business places have a personality, a rhythm, a persona, so to speak? The Shopwell supermarket at 51st Street and 2nd Avenue in Manhattan has friendly workers. They seem relaxed and they're courteous to customers, patient with even the most taxing. I like to shop there even though it's a far cry from new, shiny and elegant.

On the other hand, there's a certain fashionable department store where it's a notable event if you can find a salesperson actually interested in making a sale.

It is our feeling, fortified by observation as well as research, that the personality that prevails in the workplace is dictated from the top. Management is such an important factor. That's why talented managers are in such demand; Blanchard and Johnson pinpoint some essentials in *The One Minute Manager*. Setting goals by agreement, praising whenever genuinely possible and reprimanding without personalizing and with an eye to saving face are what they propose.†

In the total scheme of office management, creating and strengthening a positive climate is always at the forefront.

• Catch someone doing something right and praise him.

• Praise people on the way to excellence. Don't wait for perfect performance to tell them you notice.

---

*Thomas J. Peters and Robert H. Waterman, Jr., *In Search of Excellence* (New York: Harper & Row, 1982).

†Kenneth Blanchard and Spencer Johnson, *The One Minute Manager* (New York: William Morrow & Co., Inc., 1982).

- When criticism is necessary, speak to the issue at hand, not the personality, and keep to suggestions for correction and guidelines for creating checkpoints.

How to Handle Inside Squabbles

As a manager, you can't ignore infighting—nor can you dictate good feelings between the disputants. However, you can use your authority to negotiate a truce.

Jacqueline Heneage, director of real estate review and control of GTE in Stamford, Connecticut, suggests a method along the lines of that used by the police intervening in a family quarrel:

- Separate the disputants.
- Allow ventilation separately but not to each other. Listen without judgment or comment, so they can blow off steam.
- Realizing that the reasons offered as the rationale for an argument may be smoke screens for the real issues of self-esteem or status, it may be wise to impose a resolution without ascribing blame to either of the parties. They may be grateful for your intervention in a situation that's out of control.
- Make getting along a prerequisite for maintaining the job.

In my teaching days, I was on the picket line in a strike that had generated bad feelings between the teacher's union and the community, represented by the board of education. Administration was not part of the strike, and while our principal wasn't allowed to let us enter the building, even to use the facilities, he nonetheless appeared often to say hello and touch base with us, a fact that was much appreciated. On the other hand, we were angry at several teachers who had chosen not to join the strike, and they had to endure our catcalls as they came and left each day.

Eventually a settlement was reached, and we were back on the job having to negotiate over new problems as well as the old. It's not easy to deal with an emotional rift. Some teachers were so furious at the colleagues who had not walked the picket line that they started a campaign to preclude any further association or friendship.

Bob Lynch, our principal, observing the scene and correctly assessing the potential for disruption, called us together and "dictated" the terms of our future working relationships. "The strike is over," he said. "And from my point of view it's a dead issue as to who was right or wrong. Now our job is to forget it and

build goodwill again. I tell you that I will tolerate nothing less
and I'll come down heavy if I don't see a quick reconciliation."
It did the trick! He provided the *deus ex machina* we needed to
make us behave decently—and everyone, in this case, was de-
lighted to relinquish righteousness. His timing was right and he
used his authority productively to implement a good outcome for
everyone—the teachers who were at odds and, of course, those
most affected by the strike, the students.

Everyone benefited by his appropriate negotiating prowess.

Delegating Authority

A problem many women executives face is their own reluctance
to delegate authority. For various reasons, it seems to be more of
a problem for women than for men. The manager may think no
one else knows how to do the job as well as she. Or she may
fear that if the men she directs resent her they will sabotage the
effort by dragging their heels. She may be afraid of being too
soft or sounding too tough.

Lack of experience may make her insecure about her ability
to deal with people and she may get nervous if she doesn't oversee
every detail. Whatever the reason, she will be reneging on her
own responsibility as a skilled executive by getting bogged down
in detail that could be better handled by others.

A manager must learn to delegate authority so that work can
continue in an orderly fashion even if she's not on the scene. If
her style is defined by her involvement in every facet of the task
at hand, then she's not delegating sufficiently, and things will fall
apart in her absence. It may make her feel important but it serves
neither the business nor the person who mistakenly imposes such
a burden on herself. Better to face the fears of what might happen
if you relinquish some authority. If you have been retreating to
the familiar and occupying yourself with routine tasks that could
be handled by other workers, decide to delegate and free yourself
to deal with more creative pursuits.

The executive who finds it difficult to delegate authority
should do some self-negotiating.

What are your objectives? Expand them! Review your facts
and assumptions. Do some need to be revised or discarded?

What are your own needs? Safety and security, love and

belonging, self-esteem? And what do your workers need?

What type of climate have you been projecting? Boring, cold, remote, reliable, friendly? Honestly assess whether you've been making the effort to generate a positive climate. It always comes from the top down. You can make a real impact.

Everyone agreed that Frances, as office manager, made sure that things got done well and on time. The major flaw in her performance was that she was reluctant to take on new challenges. Not that she lacked ambition. But there was just so much detail that in fact she found herself staying later and later to take care of it. When her husband strongly objected to her outlandish hours, she had to speak to her boss about the problem.

The conversation they had convinced her that her problem was in the realm of delegating authority.

"Can't some of these functions be handled by your secretary?" he asked.

She realized, upon self-negotiation, that she had been expecting both too little and too much of her secretaries; a reason, perhaps, for frequent turnover.

- It was too much to expect her secretary to work the same long hours she did.
- While requiring the secretary to be present and available to do her bidding, she didn't actually give enough work of an interesting nature and she gave over no task requiring responsibility.

Whatever the psychological reasons for her own insecurity, changes had to be made and she decided to make them.

Her goals were to get the work done while cutting out much of her overtime, and still have time to engage in more creative tasks. (Objectives.)

Fact Finding: She realized her secretary was capable of doing research and handling important telephone clients.

Need for Safety and Security: She confronted her reluctance to give over some authority.

Love and Belonging: She agreed that her secretary's need for feeling important in the office was genuine.

Climate: Along with her reluctance to assign other than mundane tasks came a paucity of praise and recognition for a job well done. She corrected that as she started to take notice.

Strategy: She decided to get her secretary to participate with her in a search for excellence and to share rewarding tasks.

In taking all these things into consideration and implementing a change, her own status increased, everyone in the office benefited, and she acquired a new skill—delegating authority wisely.

Reminders:

• Be sure to explain the scope of the job you expect done and the purpose of the whole assignment. Get feedback to make sure there is understanding about expectations. Are you on the same frequency and negotiating the same subject matter?

• Be clear on deadline date and help to make a time chart to guide the segments for each step.

• Telling why you chose a person for a particular task is an affirmation which fosters a good self-image in the person, and thus improves job performance.

• When the finished product is presented give credit for the individual effort that went into its making. A grateful executive who acknowledges effort will be rewarded by dedication to the next project.

Delegating means you must relinquish some decision-making power, but it brings you input and gives the worker a stake in the result. It has been demonstrated over and over that workers can be great innovators and are often the best people to suggest changes that will affect their work for the better. Seeing oneself as more significant to total production is a spur to creativity. Thus, when you delegate you increase productivity and creativity in both yourself and your staff.

Sales and Negotiation

Unfortunately, not every salesperson knows that a sales transaction is a negotiation. When I go into a retail store to buy a coat I want to be acknowledged (not wait till a conversation ends), I want to see a variety of merchandise (not have a rack of coats pointed out), I want advice on whether it's right or a suggestion if something better is available. A salesperson should be consciously engaged in promoting the climate such attention creates.

I do not appreciate being urged, persuaded, or manipulated. Even if I buy this time, I'll look for a more hospitable atmosphere next time. Too many salespeople act as if there is no tomorrow. Negotiating skills are essential for anyone in sales.

Special Problems for Women

Commercial real estate used to be the domain of men, while residential sales staffs were heavily populated by women. The difference in the money to be made is substantial. The same applies to industrial reps and sales of technological equipment. While these more lucrative sales fields are opening up, a woman still needs to use special negotiating tactics. For instance, even if she gets a job in commercial real estate, she probably has to enlist her boss's aid to get part of the action. I know one woman who missed out repeatedly because potential clients wouldn't accept a saleswoman. A sympathetic boss helped her overcome the problem by appearing with her and substantiating her expertise. Only then was she able to establish her credibility.

The need for persistence is even greater in telephone sales. Selling a high-priced product over the phone is a process that may take months. Furthermore, one needs to become adept at bypassing secretaries who preciously guard their bosses time. Unless you establish a relationship you may not get through. The frustration you experience can produce Machiavellian schemes. One frustrated caller, upon receiving the usual "I'm sorry, he's in conference," said with gleeful malice, "Well, don't disturb him. Just tell him the results of the test are positive."

A salesperson must be skilled in closing the sale. What does it profit her if she's created a good climate and assessed the client's needs if she can't nail down the order. When she realizes from the gestures and the meta-talk that a customer is just about ready, she must try to bring the session to a close.

"Will it be the purple or the fuchsia?"

"Shall it be delivered to the apartment or your office?"

If the sale doesn't go through let the customer depart in good spirits. It's the best assurance that she'll return, next time to buy.

Negotiating Sales

The job of salesperson requires constant negotiating and as in all negotiation, the conclusion—the sale—should satisfy both parties. A good relationship leads to a long association, and nowhere is this more true than with a satisfied customer. In such a transaction certain parts of the negotiation process assume particular significance:

- *Needs*: What does she need? Your expertise, your opinion, alternatives, reassurance, guidance or just service?
- *Climate*: Even a difficult potential customer responds to a positive climate. Don't react to a careless or hostile climate in kind. If you make it a point to be disarming, more likely than not you will knock the chip off the shoulder.
- *Philosophy*: A sales situation is the perfect example of the value of the win/win philosophy since a satisfied customer is the key to future negotiations as well as a barometer of success in this one.

Conclusion

If you have come this far with us, you know by now that certain common assumptions that often prevent women from negotiating effectively are simply not true. You know that:

- A skillful woman negotiator does not have to be aggressive or hardheaded.
- You do not have to know all the tricks to negotiate completely.
- There are no absolute how-to tips that will hold true today, tomorrow and always.

Like any other art, negotiation is a process that advances in stages, is ever-changing, and is always "becoming." Not achieving immediate favorable results is not necessarily a defeat. Nor are you a failure if you satisfy only some of your objectives. The competent negotiator takes the long-range view. If she cannot obtain her objective all at once, she is willing to work toward it gradually, through many negotiations.

If you have assumed an extra workload in an effort to justify a higher salary, being denied the raise is only the opening scene in an ongoing negotiation. When you negotiate the next round, you'll find it easier to convince a superior of the legitimacy of your position if the groundwork has already been laid.

If you understand the structure of the negotiation process and try to come up with as many alternative solutions as you can, you maximize the possibilities for achieving your goals. In finding creative solutions you may even be so helpful to your opponent that he will happily agree to an outcome that benefits the both of you.

Having a philosophy in which everyone wins, and neither negotiator loses, creates the sustaining relationships that produce even smoother negotiations next time around. When negotiators learn to trust each other, results can be achieved in little time.

Women need to redefine power and to wrestle with the issue of whether they seek it and to what end. Power is not barking orders and having someone obey. Rather, power is creating situations in which people perform well together and build an atmosphere leading to continued amity. Having power, and using it to such an end, is within women's grasp. This is another reason that women should learn how to negotiate and develop the confidence to do so.

Ask yourself some essential questions before you take action in a negotiation:

• Have I expanded my objectives to the fullest?
• Have I examined my assumptions in my quest for facts?
• Do I have a clear idea of the points of disagreement?
• When I take positions, am I flexible enough so I'm not locked into them?
• Have I self-negotiated to understand the emotional basis of my behavior?
• Have I figured out my needs and those of my opponent?
• Am I making every effort to create a positive climate?
• Is the strategy I'm planning to use likely to destroy that climate?
• What is my negotiating philosophy? Is it serving me well?

When confronted with an unresolved situation, whether in a business setting or your personal life, make it your habit to negotiate through to a solution. Use the negotiation map to prepare you. You will be well fortified to deal with any opponent, even one to whom you have attributed a position of power. Even in the most difficult scenarios you will at the very least be assured of getting the best results from a poor situation.

It is said that practice makes perfect but that's not exactly true. If you do something wrong one hundred times the chances are it will be wrong on the one hundred and first. However, given the structure upon which to build your negotiating skills, practice is the final element necessary for perfection.

We may not be able to change the world, but we can function better in life if we negotiate our way through. There is no one way to do anything. The more options we discover, the more success we will have.

And that's what we wish all our readers for today and for the future.

Bibliography

Blanchard, Kenneth and Spencer Johnson. *The One Minute Manager*. New York: William Morrow & Co., 1982.

Bok, Sissela. *Secrets*. New York: Pantheon Books, 1982.

Bolles, Richard Nelson. *What Color Is My Parachute?* Berkeley, Calif: Ten Speed Press, 1982.

Bramson, Robert M., Ph.D. *Coping With Difficult People*. New York: Ballantine Books, 1981.

Burns, Dr. David. *Feeling Good: The New Mood Therapy*. New York: William Morrow & Co., 1980.

Buskerk, Richard H. and Beverly Mills. *Beating Men at Their Own Game, A Women's Guide to Successful Selling in Industry*. New York: McGraw-Hill, Inc., 1980.

Dowling, Colette. *Cinderella Complex*. New York: Summit Books, 1981.

Dyer, Wayne W. *Pulling Your Own Strings*. New York: Crowell, 1978.

Easton, Susan, Joan N. Mills and Diane Kramer Winoker. *Equal to the Task: How Working Women are Managing in Corporate America*. New York: Seaview Books, 1982.

Fenn, Margaret. *In the Spotlight*. New York: Prentice-Hall, 1980.

Friedan, Betty. *The Feminine Mystique*. New York: W. W. Norton & Co., Inc., 1963.

Gilbert, Lynn and Gaylen Moore. *Particular Passions, Talks with Women Who Have Shaped Our Lives*. New York: Clarkson N. Potter, Inc., 1981.

Gilligan, Carol. *In a Different Voice*. Cambridge: Harvard University Press, 1982.

Goodman, Ellen. *Close to Home*. New York: Simon and Schuster, 1979.

Halas, Celia and Roberta Matteson. *I've Done So Well, Why Do I Feel So Bad?* New York: Macmillan Publishing Company, 1978.

Harragan, Betty Lehan. *Games Mother Never Taught You*. New York: Warner Books, Inc., 1977.

Hennig, Margaret and Anne Jardim. *The Managerial Woman*. New York: Doubleday Publishing Co., 1977.

Hayakawa, S. I. *Language and Thought in Action*. New York: Harcourt, Brace and World, Inc., 1949.

Kanter, Rosbeth Moss. *Men and Women of the Corporation*. New York: Basic Books, 1977.

Korzybski, Alfred. *Science and Sanity*. International Non-Aristotelian Library Publishing Co. 4th ed., 1958. (Available through the Institute of General Semantics, 3029 Eastern Ave., Baltimore, Md. 21224.)

Lee, Irving J. *How to Talk With People*. Baltimore, Md.: International Society for General Semantics, 1952.

Madow, Dr. Leo. *Anger: How to Recognize and Cope with It*. New York: Scribner, 1974.

Maslow, Abraham. *Motivation and Personality*. New York: Harper and Row Publishers, Inc., 1954.

Nierenberg, Gerard I. *The Art of Creative Thinking*. New York: Simon and Schuster, 1982.

Nierenberg, Gerard I. *Fundamentals of Negotiating*. New York: Hawthorne, 1973.

Nierenberg, Gerard I. and Henry Calero. *How to Read a Person Like a Book*. New York: Simon and Schuster, 1971.

Nierenberg, Gerard I. and Henry Calero. *Meta–Talk*. New York: Simon and Schuster, 1981.

Nierenberg, Roy A. and Jonathan Llwellyn. *The Art of Negotiation Computer Preparation Program*. Experience in Software, 1984.

Pearson, Carol and Katherine Pope. *The Female Hero in American and British Literature*. New York: R. R. Bowker Co., 1981.

Peters, Thomas J. and Robert H. Waterman, Jr. *In Search of Excellence*. New York: Harper and Row Publishers Inc., 1982.

Reaves, Chuck. *The Theory of 21*. New York: M. Evans and Co., 1983.

Russianoff, Penelope. *Why Do I Think I'm Nothing Without a Man?* New York: Bantam Books, 1982.

Rubin, Dr. Theodore. *The Angry Book*. New York: Macmillan Publishing Co., 1970.

Sarnoff, Dorothy. *Make the Most of Your Best*. New York: Doubleday Publishing Co., 1981.

Seaford, Tschirhart and Mary Ellen Donovan. *Women and Self Esteem*. New York: Doubleday Publishing Co., 1984.

Shainess, Natalie. *Sweet Suffering*. New York: The Bobbs Merrill Co., Inc., 1984.

Siegelman, Ellen Y. *Personal Risk*. New York: Harper and Row Publishers, Inc., 1984.

Smith, Manuel J., Ph.D. *When I Say No, I Feel Guilty*. New York: Bantam Books, 1975.

Tavris, Carol. *Anger, The Misunderstood Emotion*. New York: Simon and Schuster, 1983.

Williams, Marcille Gray. *The New Executive Woman*. New York: The New American Library Inc., 1977.

Index